SPIELMAN'S ORIGINAL

Scroll Saw Patterns

Patrick & Patricia Spielman

 Sterling Publishing Co., Inc.   New York

Edited by Timothy Nolan

Library of Congress Cataloging-in-Publication Data
Spielman, Patrick E.
    [Original scroll saw patterns]
    Spielman's original scroll saw patterns / by Patrick and Patricia
Spielman.
        p.   cm.
    ISBN 0-8069-7214-9
    1. Jig saws.   2. Woodwork.   I. Spielman, Patricia.
TT186.S675   1990
684'.083—dc20   89-49314
                                                    CIP

                        3   5   7   9   10   8   6   4

Copyright © 1990 by Patrick and Patricia Spielman
Published by Sterling Publishing Co., Inc.
387 Park Avenue South, New York, N.Y. 10016
Distributed in Canada by Sterling Publishing
% Canadian Manda Group, P.O. Box 920, Station U
Toronto, Ontario, Canada M8Z 5P9
Distributed in Great Britain and Europe by Cassell PLC
Artillery House, Artillery Row, London SW1P 1RT, England
Distributed in Australia by Capricorn Ltd.
P.O. Box 665, Lane Cove, NSW 2066
Manufactured in the United States of America
All rights reserved
Sterling ISBN 0-8069-7214-9 Paper

DEDICATION

To Mr. and Mrs. Vern E. Rogers and to
the memory of Mr. and Mrs. Andrew M. Spielman,
our parents, with thanks for their love and support.

Contents

Introduction   6

PATTERNS

Penguins   18

Small Cutouts   20

Lambs   22

Jack In The Box   23

Indian   24

Mice   25

Toy Cutouts   27

Teddy Bears   30

Musical Cutouts   32

Wildlife   36

Dinosaurs   55

Sports Figures & Dancers   64

Cows and Horses   75

Cats, Dogs, and Bunnies   80

Viking Ship   97

Southwestern Cutouts   99

Christmas Angel   105

Mushrooms   106

Bumble Bee   108

Airplane   109

Butterflies   110

Fruit   112

Frog   116

Feathered Friends   117

Fish and Sea Life   154

Flowers and Leaves   174

Mobiles   183

Frame Cutouts   193

Fretted Cutouts   210

Wastebasket and Lamp   213

About the Authors   222

Current Books by Patrick Spielman   222

Index   224

Color section follows page 128

Introduction

In the last decade and a half, scroll sawing has grown to become woodworking's most popular activity. There are several factors contributing to the increased participation and overall success of scroll sawing in general. Most importantly, the century old concept of the constant tension blade principle in scroll saw design has been dramatically refined through sound engineering and the employment of space-age materials.

Today, anyone can afford a good scroll saw. The cheapest and worst performing of the constant tension machines available today are dramatic improvements over the old school-shop-type jigsaws, namely, those saws available from the early 1930's through the mid-1970's, that never really became very popular in the private woodworking shop. See *Scroll Saw Fretwork Techniques and Projects* (Sterling Publishing Co., Inc., New York, 1990) for a comprehensive overview on the history of scroll sawing.

Another reason scroll sawing has become easier and more fun is the emergence of the office copy machine. This device has made it a snap to reproduce scroll saw patterns

Illus. 1. Patterns can be enlarged or reduced to any size with an office copy machine.

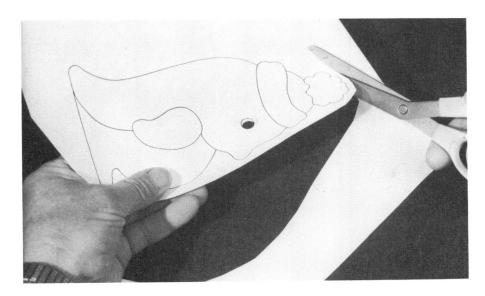

quickly and inexpensively. Pattern copies can also be enlarged or reduced to practically any predetermined size on many machines (Illus. 1 and 2). Copiers are becoming more and more sophisticated and accessible. Most public libraries have them, as do most quick printing establishments, for individuals to use. Many businesses and schools, even in remote areas, often make them available for public use on a cost per copy basis. Pattern copies of any size can now be made in just seconds for pennies a copy. Gone are such labor-intensive and crude copying and enlarging techniques as graph grids, difficult-to-adjust pantographs, and tracings made with illuminated projection devices.

Now that technology has given us good sawing devices and cheap, quick pattern copies, all that is needed is an easy, speedy, and accurate method of transferring the pattern to the work piece to ready it for sawing. To satisfy this important requirement, we highly recommend a special spray adhesive with temporary bonding qualities, available at most photography stores and studios, as well as art supply stores.

Illus. 3. Applying a very light mist of spray adhesive just to the back of the pattern.

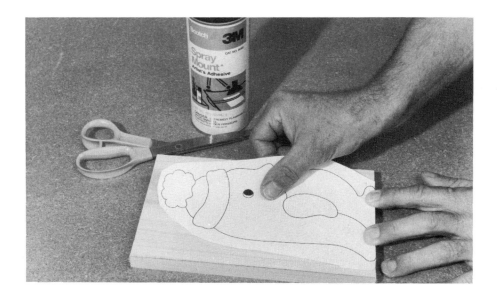

Illus. 4. Touching down the adhesive coated pattern onto the work piece. Note, in this case, the bottom straight edge of the pattern is aligned with the previously sawn edge of the wood.

Illus. 5. If working from a large board, make a rough cut first to reduce the piece to a more workable size.

To use the spray adhesive, simply apply a very light mist to the back of the pattern copy only (Illus. 3). Wait 15 to 30 seconds, press the pattern copy onto the wood with your hand and presto! you're ready to begin sawing (Illus. 4 and 5). The adhesive is the perfect temporary bond to hold the pattern to the wood throughout sawing (Illus. 6). With the pattern directly copied and applied onto the wood nothing is lost or degraded in the line transferring process and, one of the best features of this adhesive is that when sawing is completed, the pattern is easily peeled off (Illus. 7).

Spray adhesive leaves virtually no residue on the wood that might inhibit subsequent finishing. We feel obligated, supposedly by tradition, to sand the wood surface with just a few strokes of 220 grit abrasive before finishing, but it's really doubtful if this is even necessary.

Thanks to these improvements, scroll sawing has been lifted to new levels of pleasure. Now, it is not only easier but more fun for people of all ages. To help carry this joy 'further we have provided a fresh, new selection of scroll saw patterns in this book to complement those of our other pattern

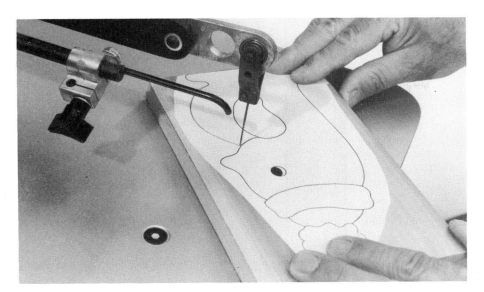

Illus. 6. Most modern scroll saws permit making very sharp turns very easily. Consequently, the entire object can be made with one continuous cut by sawing right on or along the line without interruption.

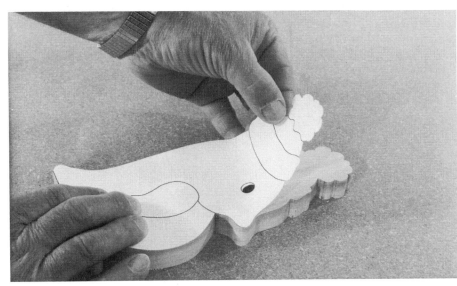

Illus. 7. When sawing is completed, the pattern lifts off the wood easily and cleanly, leaving no residue to interfere with subsequent finishing.

books, including the new *Scroll Saw Country Patterns* (Sterling Publishing Co., Inc., New York, 1990). The patterns feature fine, crisp lines with extra shading so you will know where and where not to drill or saw. This will help to relieve eye strain and contribute to easier and more accurate cutting. The 262 patterns (in 30 different categories) provide an adequate selection of patterns and fresh designs in an economical package. The projects range from fairly simple ones to those of an intermediate challenge level, overall falling somewhere in difficulty between those in *Scroll Saw*

Pattern Book (Sterling Publishing Co., New York, 1986) and our book, *Scroll Saw Fretwork Patterns* (Sterling Publishing Co., New York, 1990) prepared with professional scroll sawyer James Reidle.

To help utilize scroll saw patterns more fully, there are many ways in which a single pattern example can be worked. This will multiply the value of this book and the number of projects you can make with one pattern. Think about using various pattern designs as wall hangings, shelf or mantel decorations, door stops, tree or window ornaments, paper weights, key

Illus. 8. Pattern lines can be detailed by painting, inking, or wood burning.

Illus. 9. Paint markers (available from hobby and model shops) can be used to add a touch of color without the usual mess associated with regular paint and brushes.

Illus. 10. Examples of saw-kerf detailing on the ear and legs. In some cases you can saw away a part; then glue it back in place.

chains, miniatures and jewelry, refrigerator magnets, or just add pegs or hooks to hang things on. The designs can also be used as overlay or pierced decorations glued onto plaques, cabinet doors and panels, jewelry boxes and ornamentation on wood signs, to name just a few more application possibilities. Flip-flop the design or cut a pair and make a row of the same pattern. For even more variety, cut the same pattern from different materials.

Most all of the patterns can be sawn (Illus. 5 and 6) from materials of your choice of species, type, and thickness. For your information, we have indicated the materials we used to make the projects that are illustrated in the color section, but these are only suggestive. Where specific dimensions or finishes are important to a project pattern, they are included. Other-

wise, all the details pertaining to materials, and so on, are your preference and personal choice. For example, pages 78–79 show a horse head sawn from 2-inch-thick butternut, but this project can also be sawn from pine, mahogany, or any solid wood or from a plywood in any thickness from 1/32 inch to 2¾ inch or more—whatever is your preference or dictated by your scroll saw capacity.

Some of the line details given on the pattern can be created or produced in several different ways. One method is wood burning (Illus. 8). Painted or sealed wood may be lined with ink, and details and coloring can also be accomplished with soft-tip paint markers (Illus. 9).

An effective technique for some patterns is to use the scroll saw to cut a detailing line through the thickness of the work piece. A typical example is the elephant project

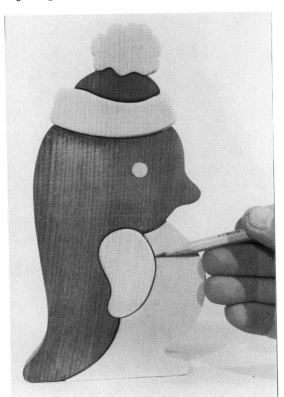

Illus. 11. All of these parts were sawn from a single piece of pine. The corners were rounded slightly with sandpaper and the parts stained different colors; then glued back to their original position.

Illus. 12. Here's another interesting possibility. The parts are cut from one piece of wood and finished independently before mounting them onto glass with hot-melt adhesive. The assembly is then set under another layer of glass. Leaving the parts slightly spaced enhances the dimensional segmentation.

11

shown in Illus. 10. Notice how the ear and leg lines are defined with saw cuts. Other techniques involve cutting a pattern into various parts, then gluing them back together (Illus. 11 and 12).

Piercing and *inside cutting* are necessary techniques for cutting out openings and other types of line-work detailing. The eye and ear line details of the bear in Illus. 13 is a good example of pierced line-work detailing. This class of work requires drilling very small holes as required to permit the blade (no. 4 or 5) to be threaded through the work (Illus. 14 and 15). Once

the blade is again clamped on each end in the machine and tensioned, sawing can proceed as usual until the inside opening work is completed. Piercing is an effective technique for removing an inside waste piece, cutting out specific parts of the project (Illus. 16 and 17) or just to cut a sawn line for adding detail to the project. Illus. 18 shows attractive sculptural-inlay projects made by rounding over the edges of pierce-cut parts, then reinserting them into the original surrounding background board.

Stack cutting, or plural sawing, involves layering two or more pieces on top of each

Illus. 13. Note the eye and ear line-work detailing accomplished by piercing.

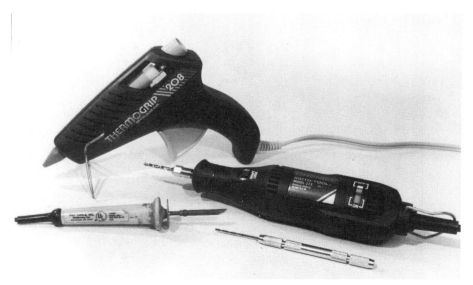

Illus. 14. Some helpful tools; top left, hot-melt glue gun; left, burning tool; right, power drill; bottom right, pin vise with a very small bit.

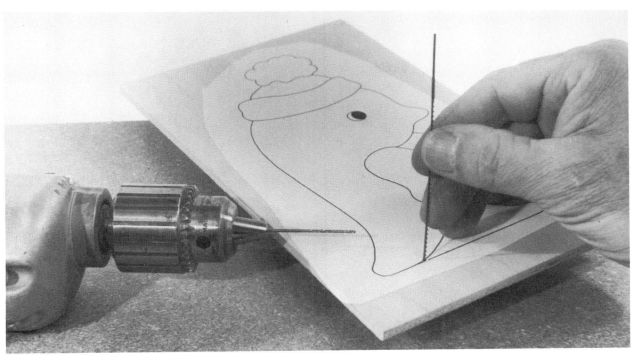

Illus. 15. To make piercing cuts, a small hole is drilled to permit the blade to be threaded through the work piece. A corner location for a hole is usually less noticeable than one drilled along a curve or uninterrupted line. This will be a child's inlay puzzle.

Illus. 16. Some of the various ways to utilize a single pattern. Left to right: Two painted cutouts, wood-burned detailing, spaces made by sawing along each side of fattened patterned lines, and an inlay puzzle sawn from ¼-inch plywood.

other and sawing them simultaneously (Illus. 19). This results in perfectly identical sawn parts. This is a good technique to employ to increase production. The essential requirement is that the work pieces be temporarily secured to each other so they don't slip around during sawing.

Various methods of stack cutting are used. Nailing in the waste area (if you have one) works well when sawing thicker size stock (Illus. 19). Spot gluing (Illus. 20), with just a little hot melt permits later separation (Illus. 21). Double-faced tape is also handy and if you don't have any, you can

Illus. 17 (left). A closer look at a colorful inlay puzzle. This is made from two layers of ¼-inch plywood. The parts are cut free from the top layer and the surrounding stock is glued to the backing layer.

Illus. 18 (below). Two examples of sculptured inlay work. The sawn pieces are slightly rounded before re-assembly. The one at the left is set flush to the background, and the design at the right is raised in relief (¼ inch) above the surrounding area.

Illus. 19. Stack sawing three layers of different woods nailed together at once. Each cut part will be exactly identical in shape.

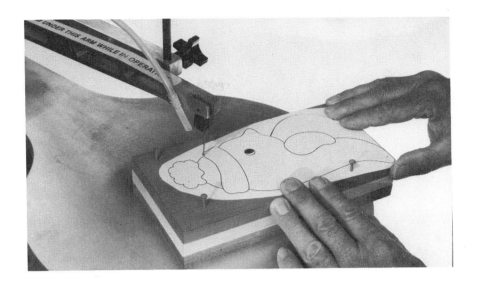

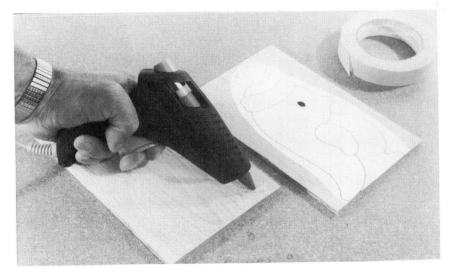

Illus. 20. Another technique of holding pieces together for stack cutting is the use of hot-melt adhesive applied to the waste areas of each layer.

Illus. 21. The result of stack sawing three layers of different woods. The cut pieces were interchanged and glued together before applying a clear finish.

15

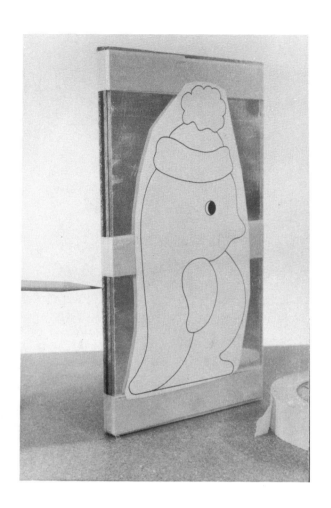

make your own. Simply use scraps of paper coated on both sides with spray adhesive. This technique works great for holding layers together of all materials, including those too thin to nail effectively. This self-made tape has more than sufficient sheer strength so the layers do not slip. However, it has a very low peel resistance which allows the layers to be separated very easily when through sawing. Commercially produced double-faced tape has a very aggressive tack and occasionally leaves some sticky stuff on the surface that sometimes will pull fibres and splinters up with it. In some situations masking tape, filament tape or other types can be wrapped around stacked pieces (Illus. 22).

A lot of creative projects can be produced

Illus. 22 (left). Stacking mirrored plastic with wood of the same thickness to produce identical pieces. Note that masking tape is used to hold all the layers together.

Illus. 23 (below). Dramatic examples of colorful mirrored plastic and solid wood inlaid into each other.

combining stack cutting and piercing into one operation. One material can thus be inlaid into another (Illus. 23). Experimentation in layering entirely different kinds of materials together for simultaneous sawing can produce some dramatic projects. For example, interchanging the sawn out mirrored plastic and stack-sawn wood parts of the same thickness with the background, new projects result in some very interesting effects (Illus. 23 and 24).

Hopefully, these ideas and tips will inspire you to get more out of the projects and patterns in this book. Once you learn to look at a pattern as a vehicle to be used in many different ways (Illus. 25), the value and use of each pattern multiplies many fold.

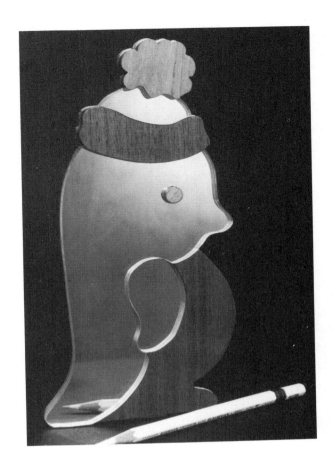

Illus. 24 (right). The use of mirrored plastic and wood adds to the visual impact.

Illus. 25 (below). Ribbons, yarn, colorful strings, and the like can often be hung or glued on to dress up a project.

Penguins

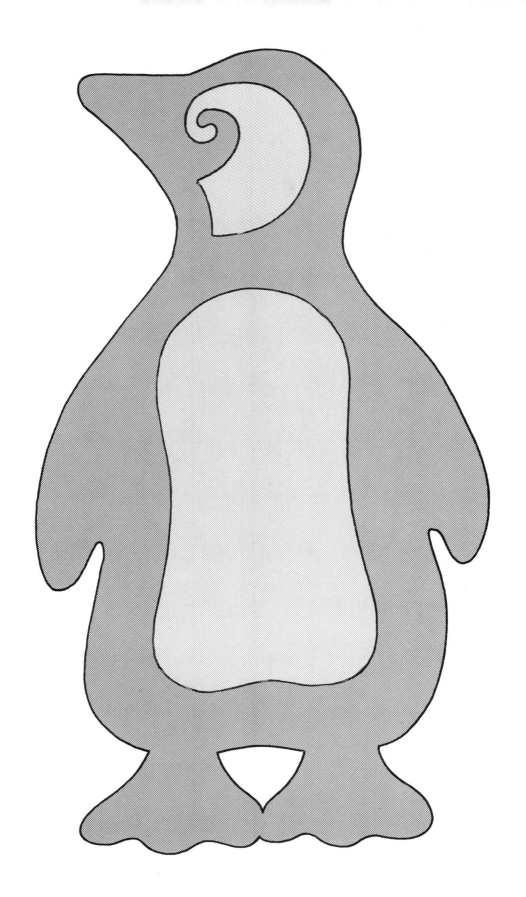

Small Cutouts

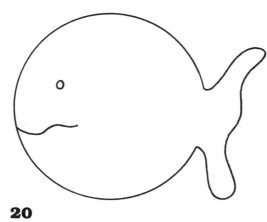

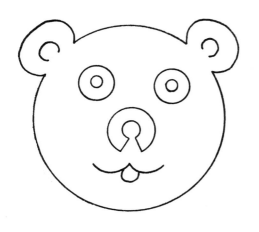

Lambs

Indian

Teddy Bears

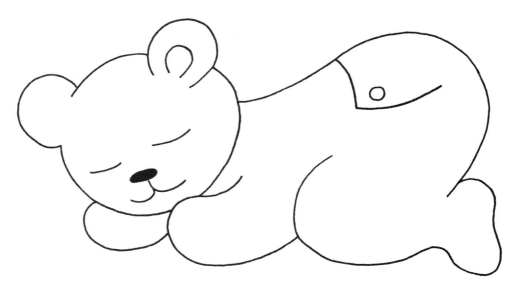

Musical Cutouts

Wildlife

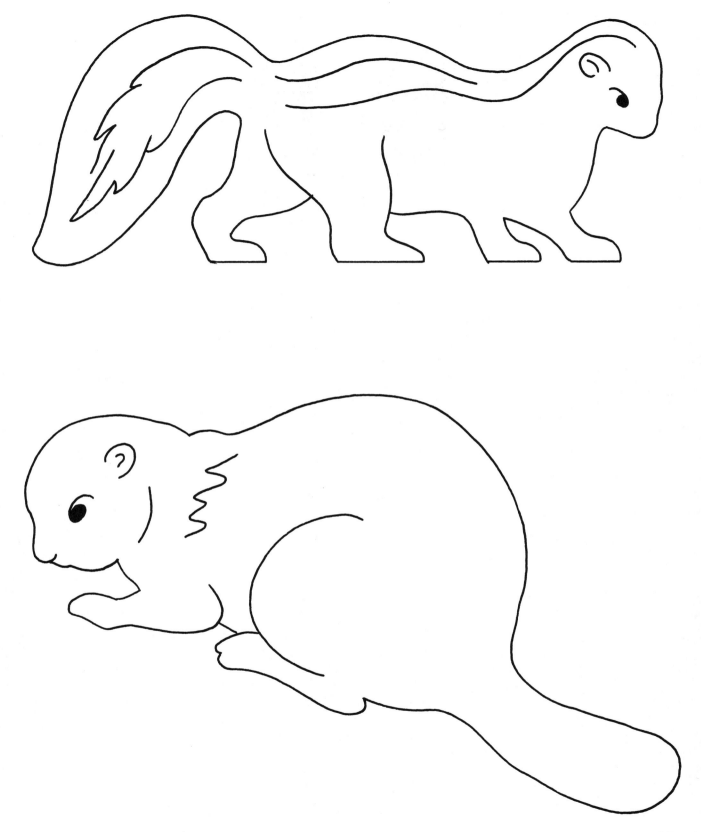

38

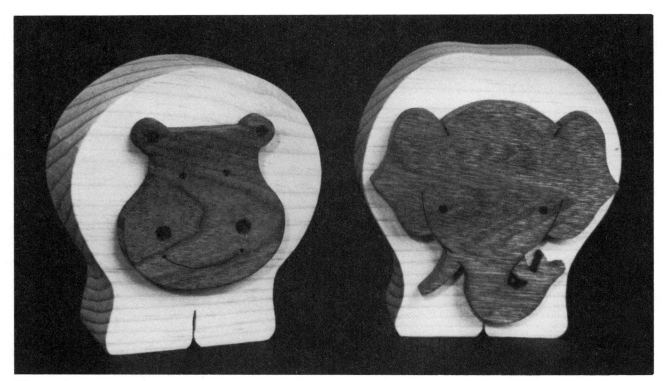

These characters (as others) can be fitted with miniature musical movements having self contained batteries activated by just the touch of a finger.

Touch-and-play musical movements are fitted into the rear of the cut outs.

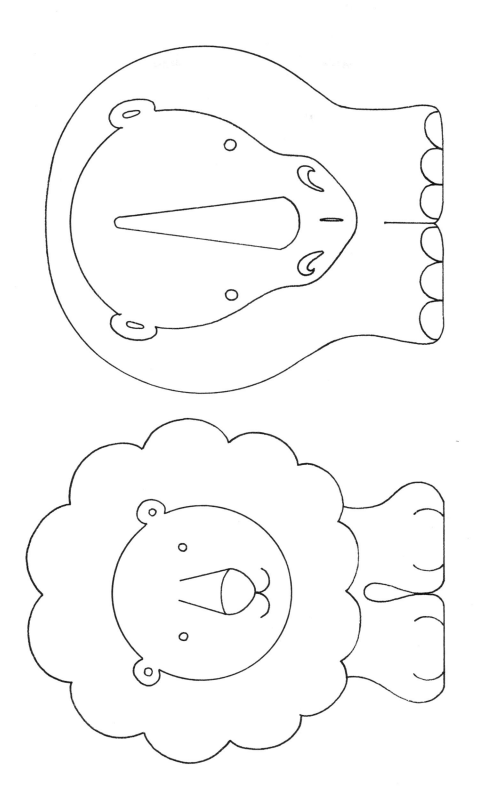

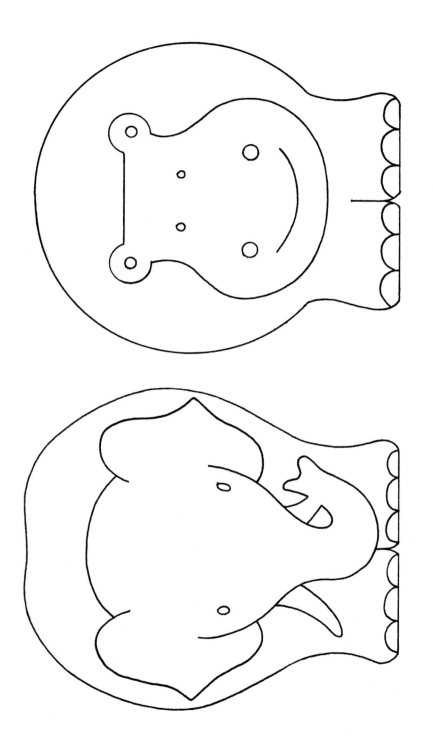

The touch-and-play compact musical movements are held in place with a bead of hot-melt glue.

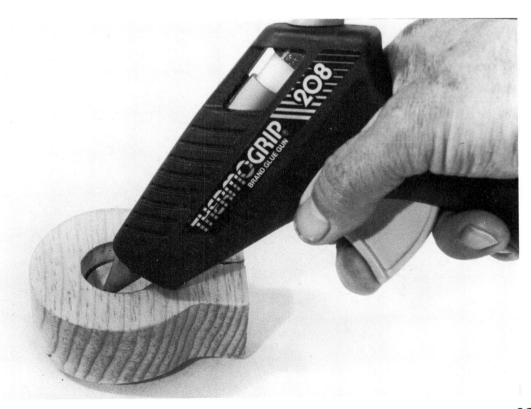

Elephant with simple sawn-line detailing.

The forward-sculptured parts are glued onto another thickness of the same wood.

48

49

50

Simple, stylized ram cut from hardwood plywood.

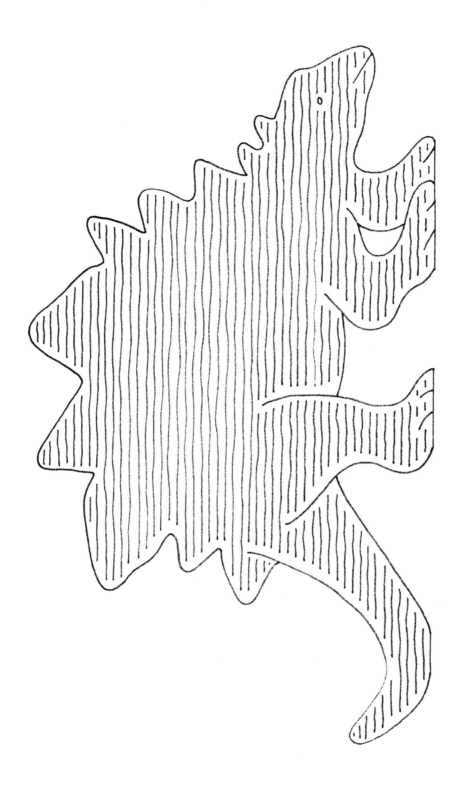

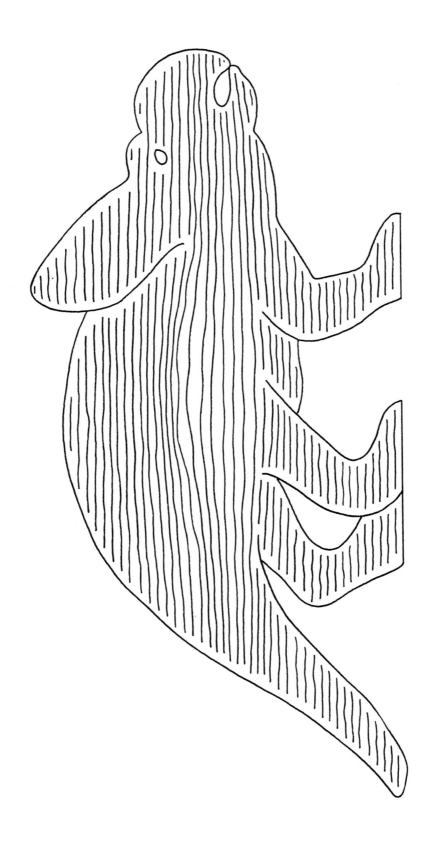

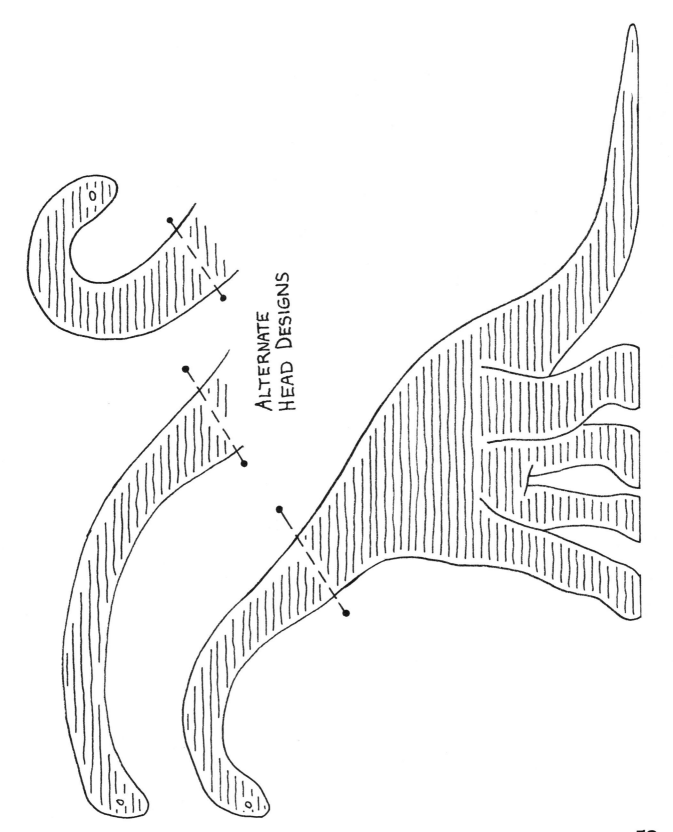

ALTERNATE
HEAD DESIGNS

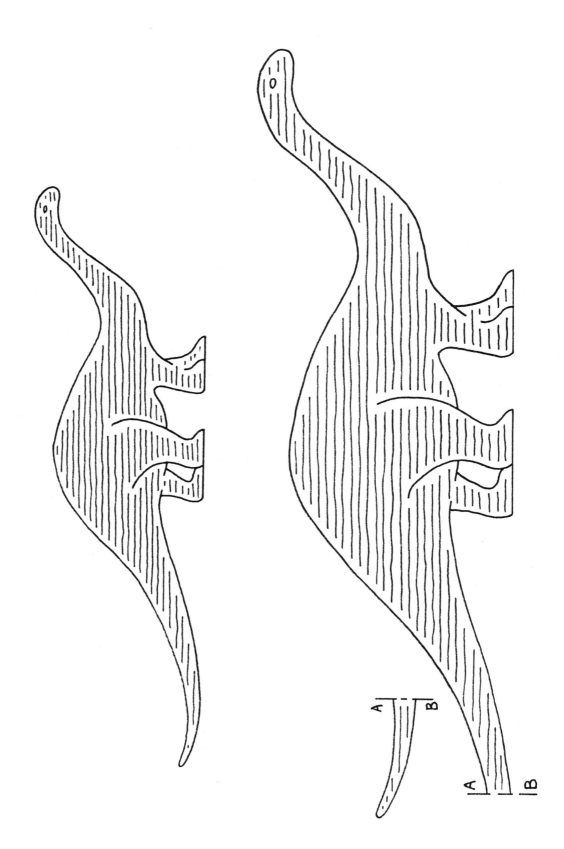

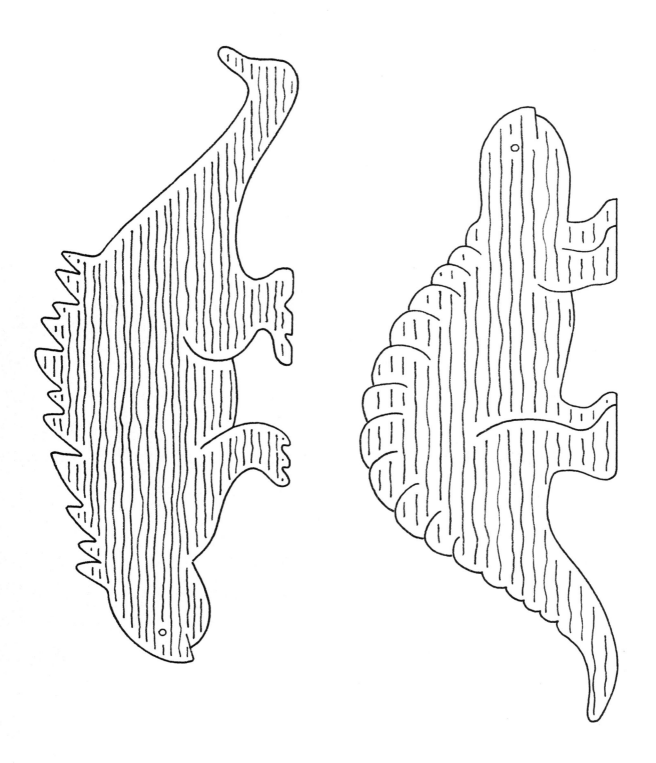

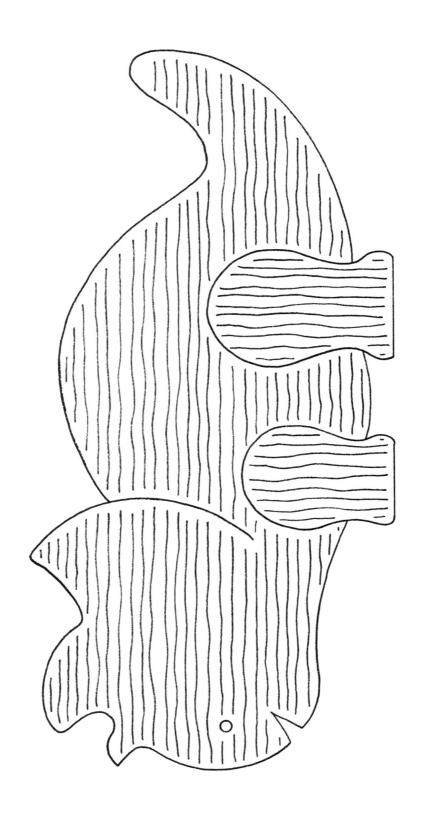

63

Sports Figures & Dancers

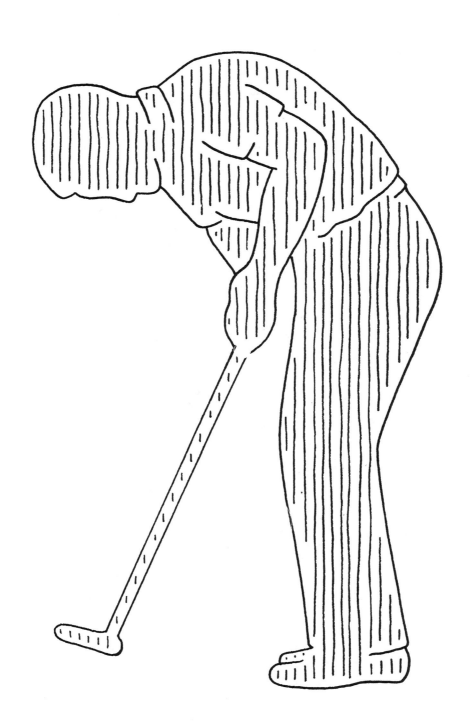

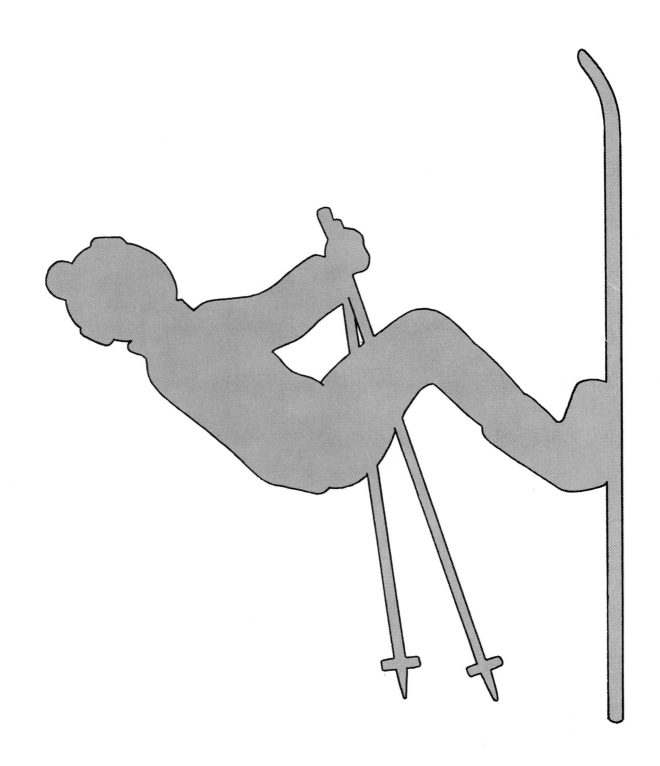

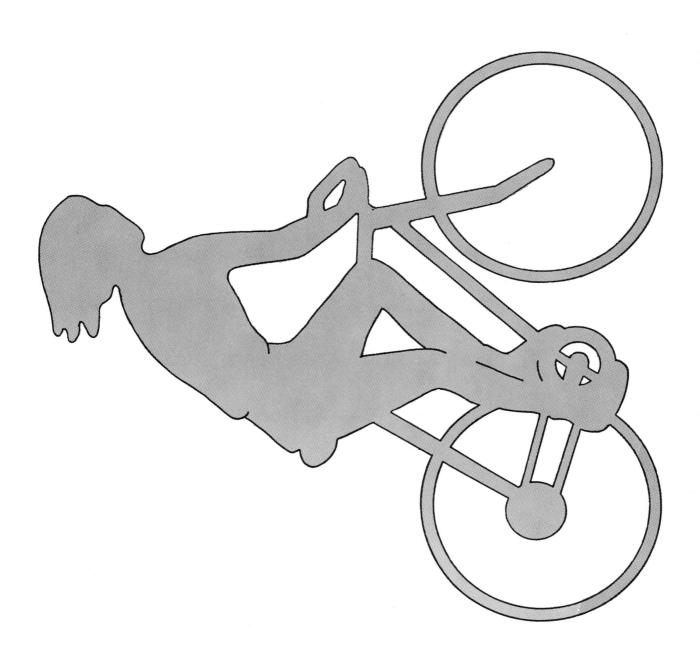

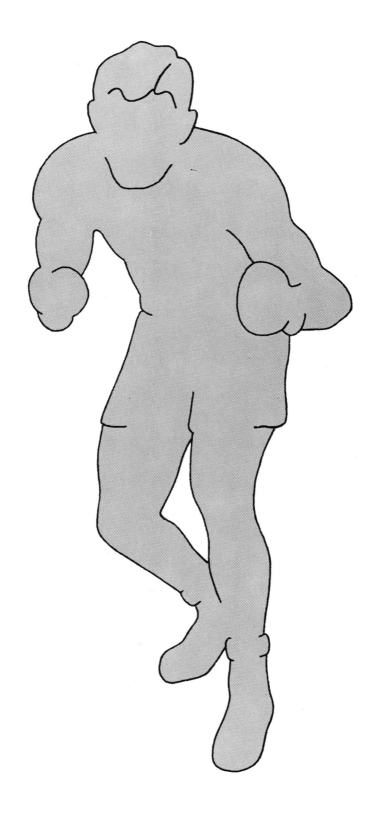

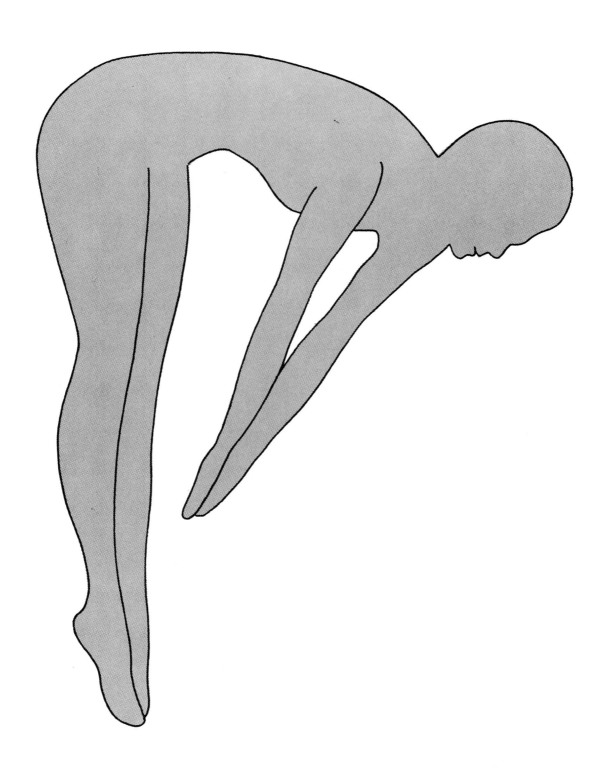

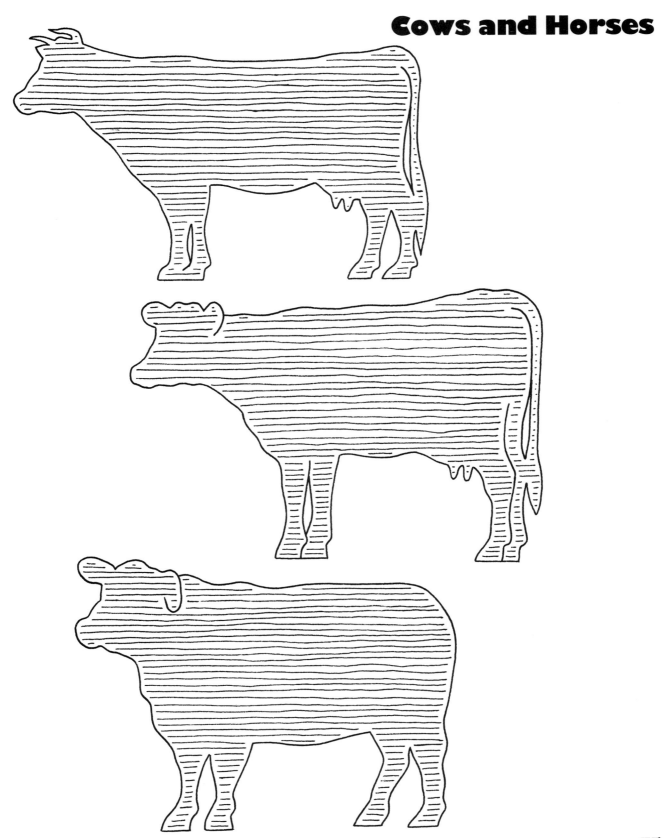

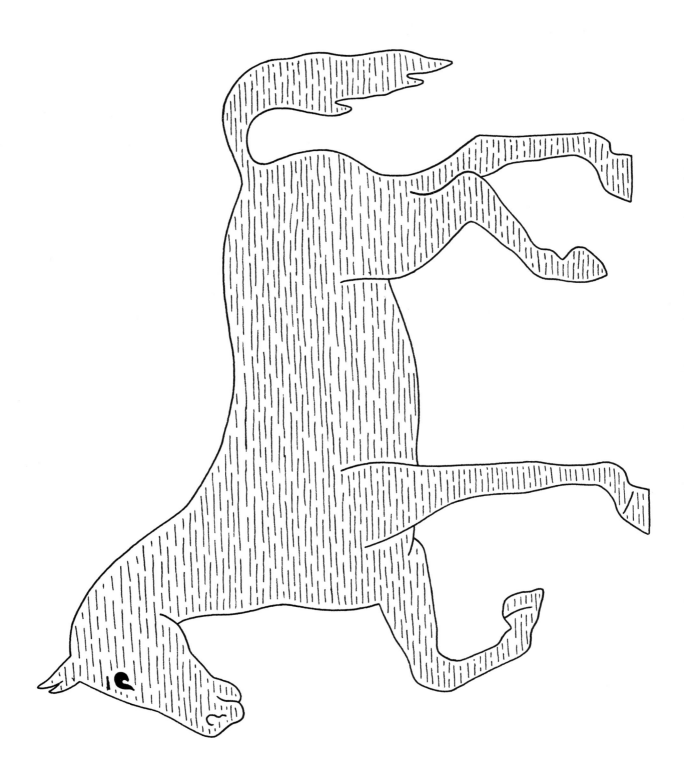

This particular decorative horse head was sawn from 2-inch-thick butternut, but other materials can be used.

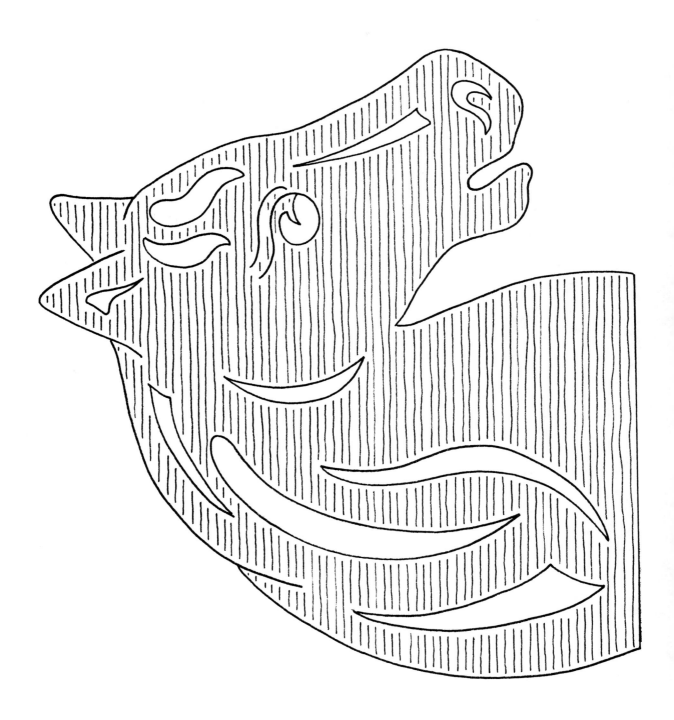

Cats, Dogs, and Bunnies

*Scottie with acrylic
painted ribbon.*

Cat and ball features sawn-line work detailing.

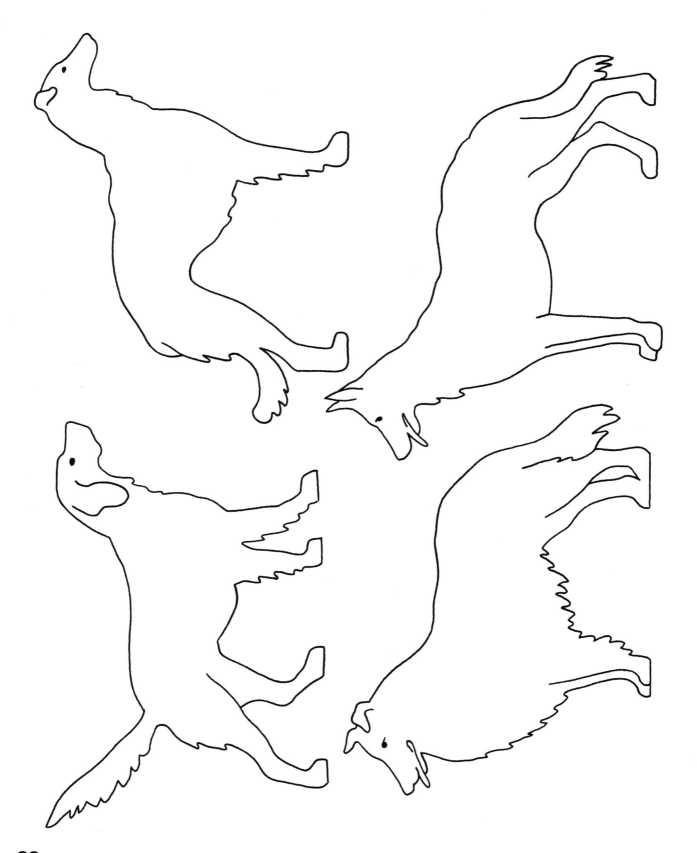

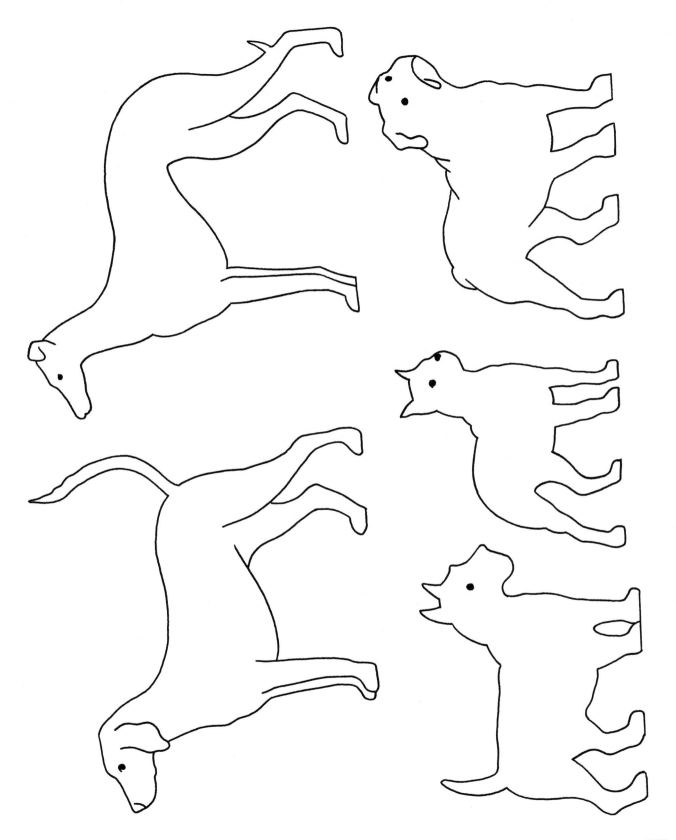

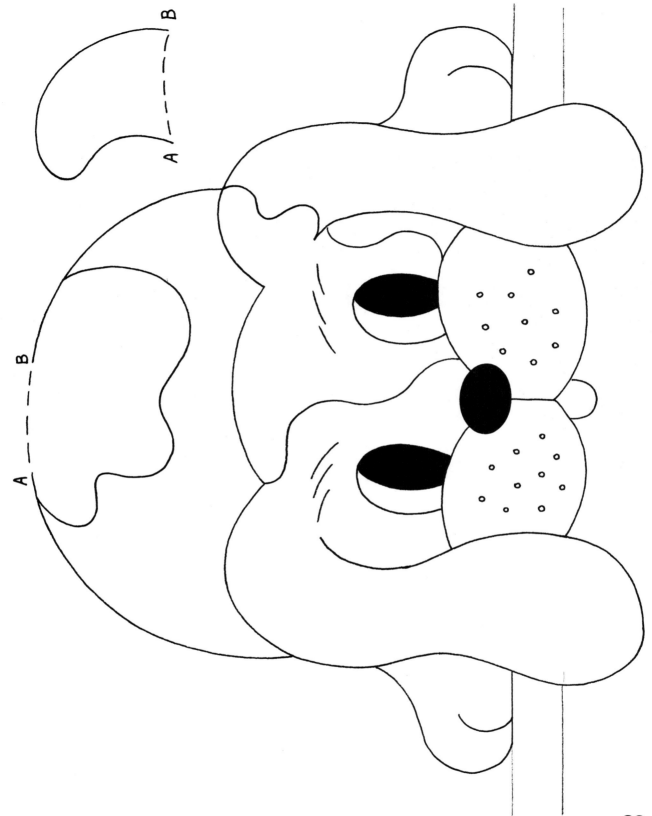

93

96

98

Southwestern Cutouts

Southwestern-inspired designs cut from solid woods ⅝-inch and ¾-inch thick.

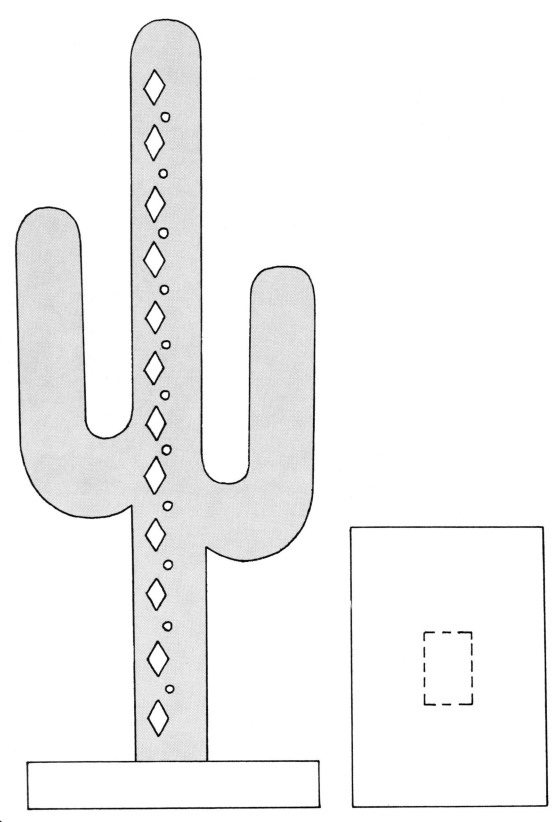

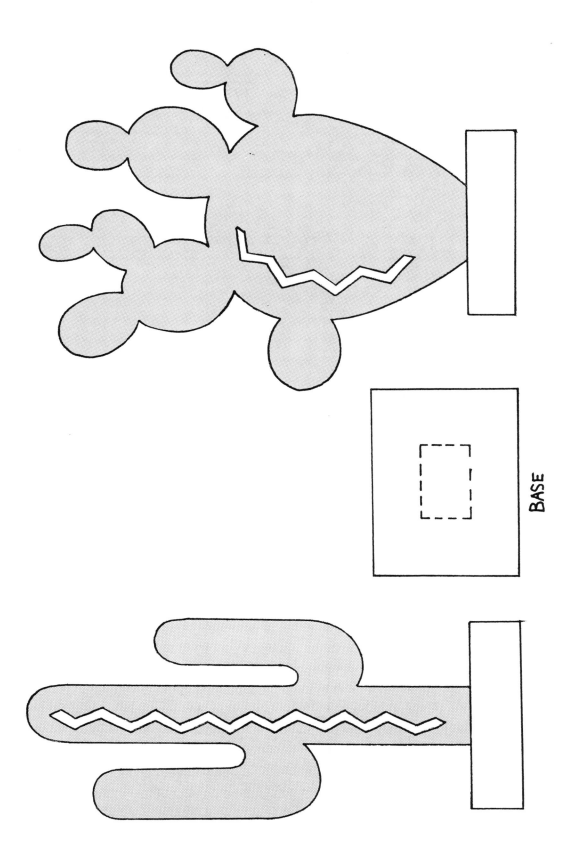

BASE

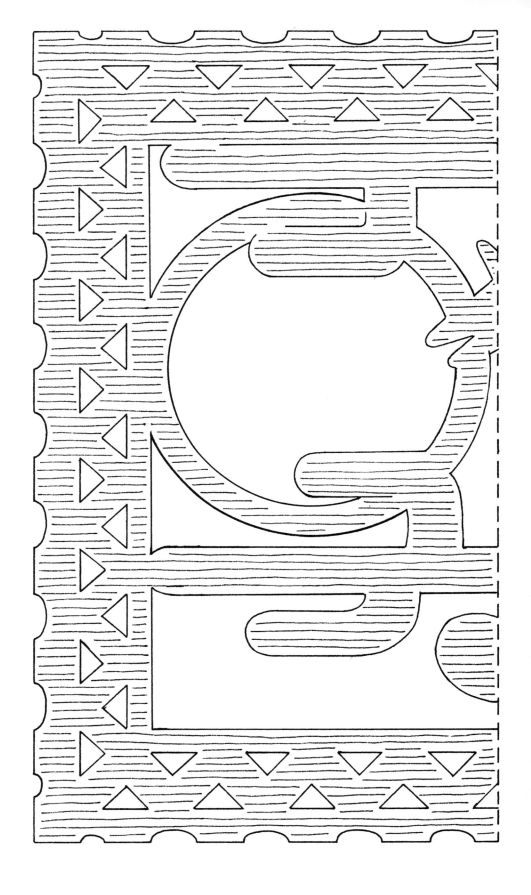

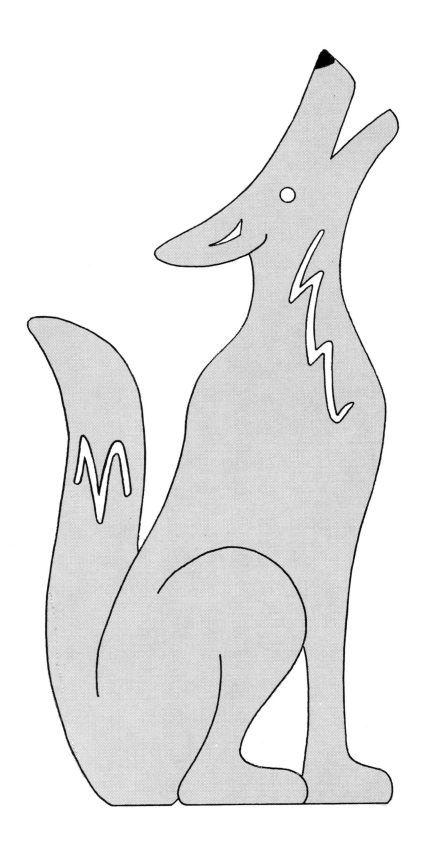

Christmas Angel

Angel. Wings from ¼-inch plywood glued to ¾-inch plywood body.

105

Mushrooms

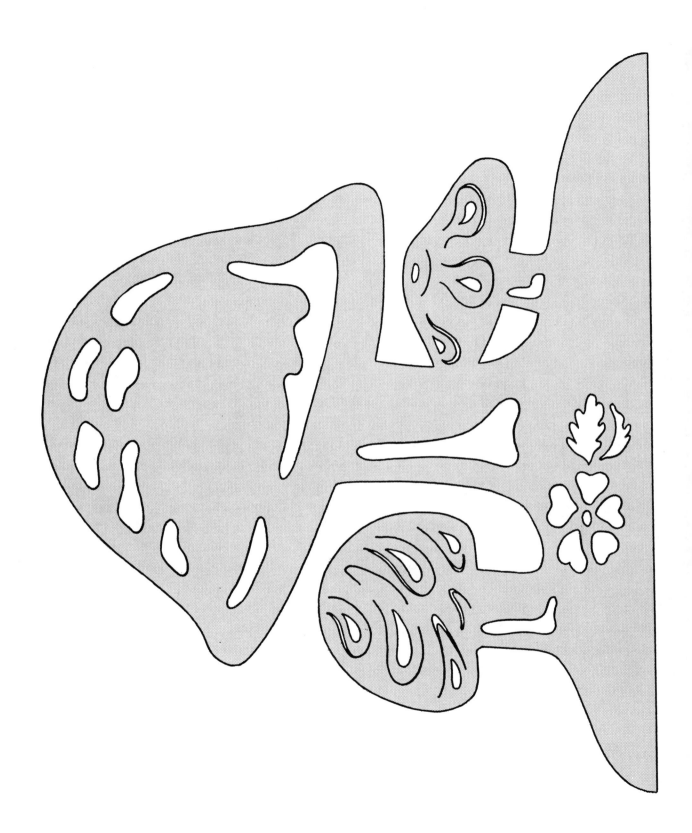

Bumble Bee

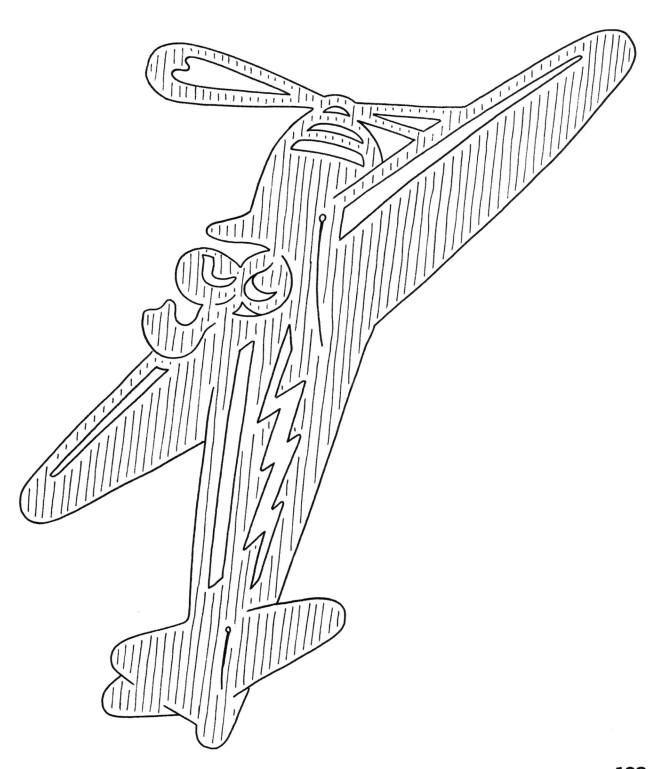

Butterflies

Fruit

Fretted-fruit cut from ¾-inch solid wood with a natural oil finish.

Frog

Feathered Friends

Mother Goose sawn from ¾-inch solid poplar and
decorated with acrylic colors.

120

Flamingo, pattern 1

Flamingo, pattern 2

Fretted rooster sawn from ¼-inch plywood.

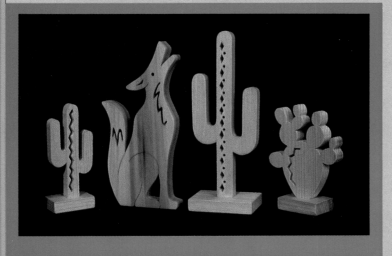

Illus. A1. Pine and poplar ⅝" and ¾" thick with natural oil finish.

Illus. A2. Fretted work in Baltic birch plywood ½" in thickness.

Illus. A3. Musical movements are inset into the rear of these whimsical creatures sawn from 1¼"-thick pine, with ¼"-thick butternut overlays.

A

Illus. B1. Three-quarter-inch poplar with part natural finish and part pigmented acrylic detailing.

Illus. B2. Hanging cat design that can be cut from stock of any convenient thickness.

Illus. B3. Hanging mobiles are easy to make. Thin plywood, turned or purchased wood balls, some fish line, toothpicks and a drop of glue are all that is required.

Illus. C1. Fretted work in Baltic birch plywood ½″ in thickness.

Illus. C2. Angel from two layers of Baltic birch plywood ¼″ and ¾″ in thickness.

Illus. C3. Cat mobile. See Illus. B3.

C

Illus. D1. Left: Fragmented and sculptured butternut overlaid and glued to a thicker, solid butternut backing. Right: Basic profile cutout with effective detailing produced with simple saw cuts.

Illus. D2. Fretted fruit cut from ¾″-thick solid stock.

Illus. D3. Fretted work in Baltic birch plywood ½″ in thickness.

D

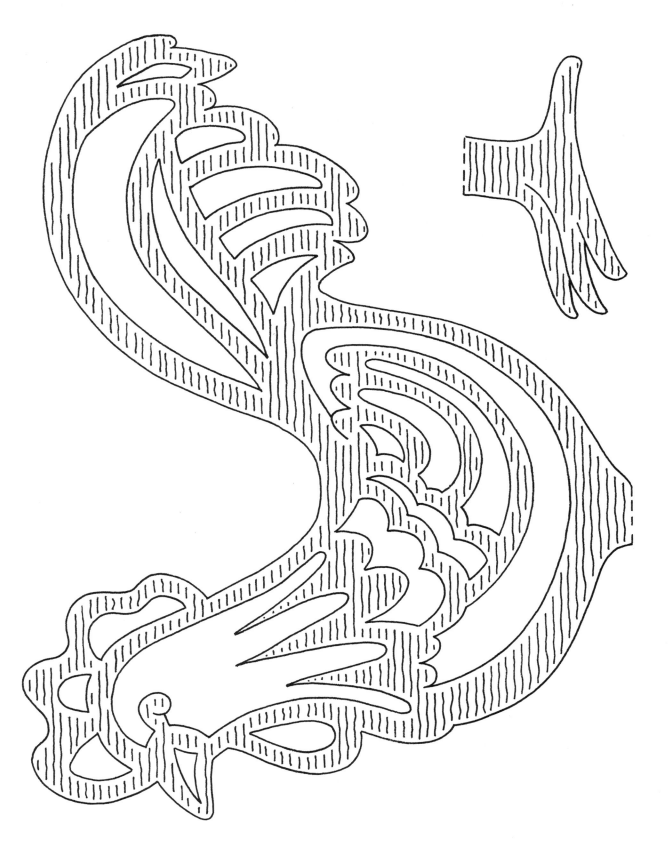

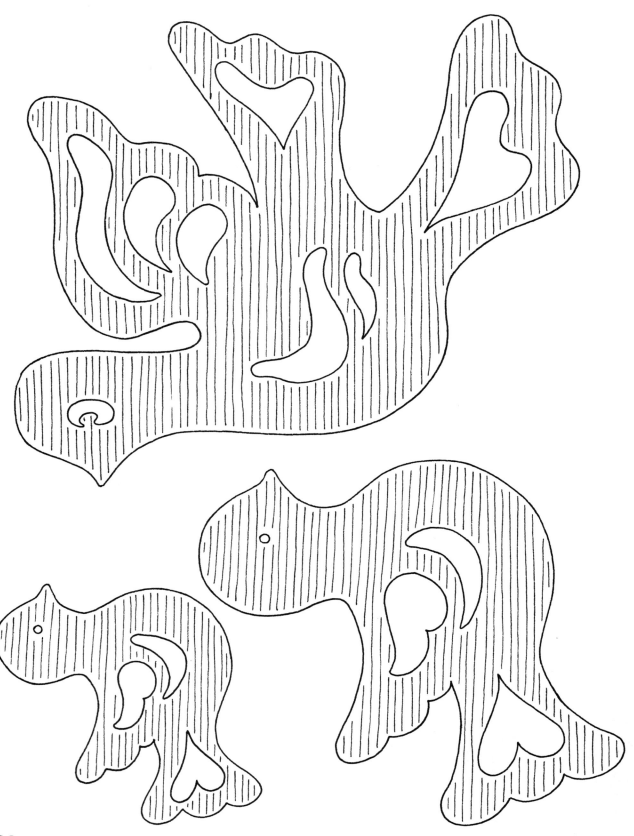

130

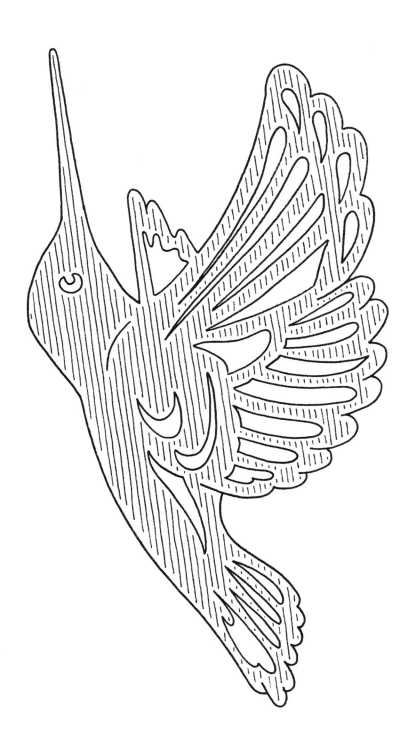

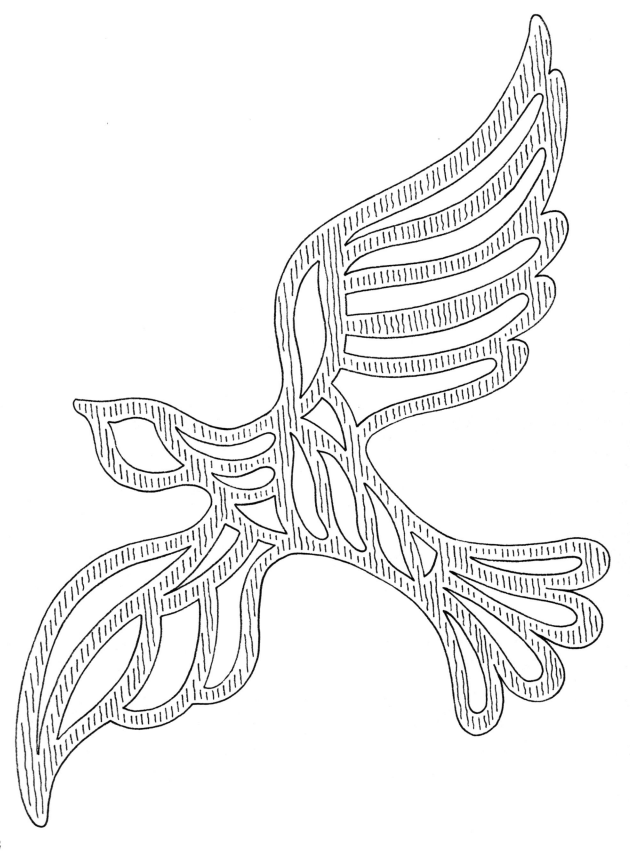

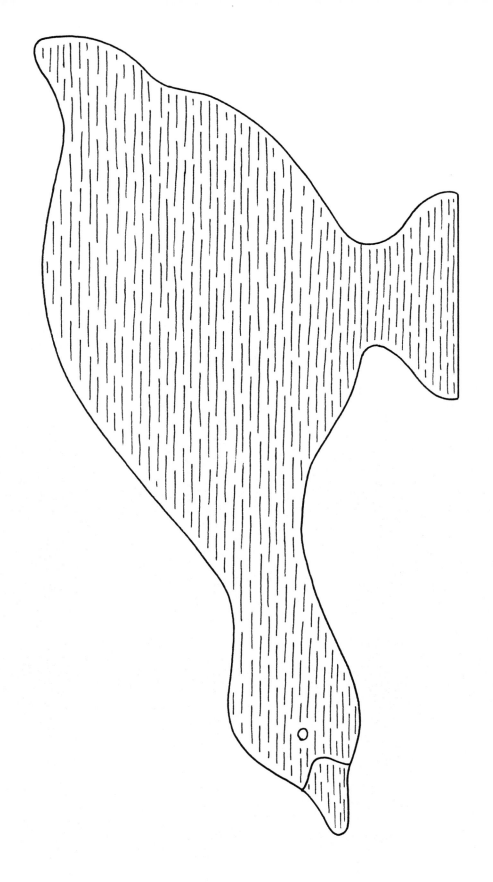

Stylized geese from ½-inch thick plywood.

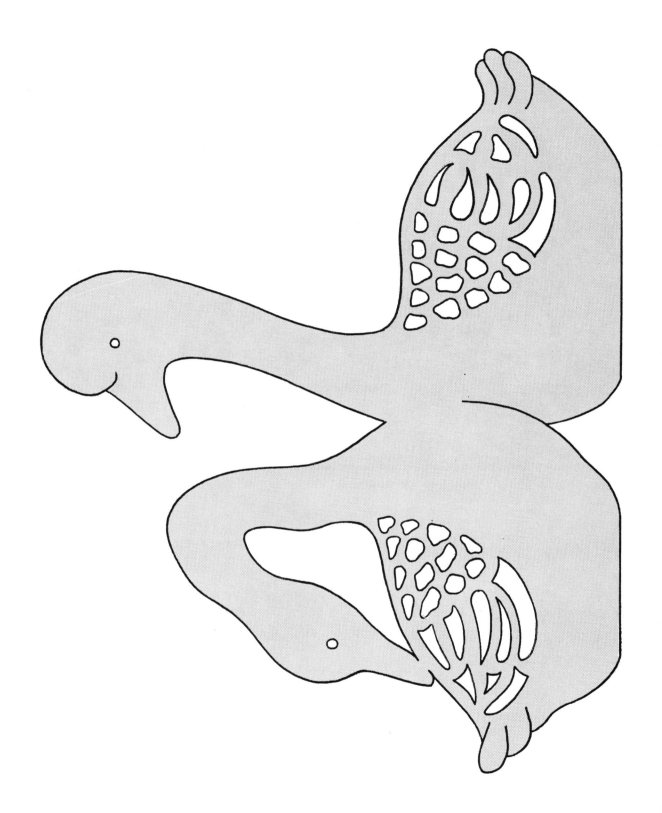

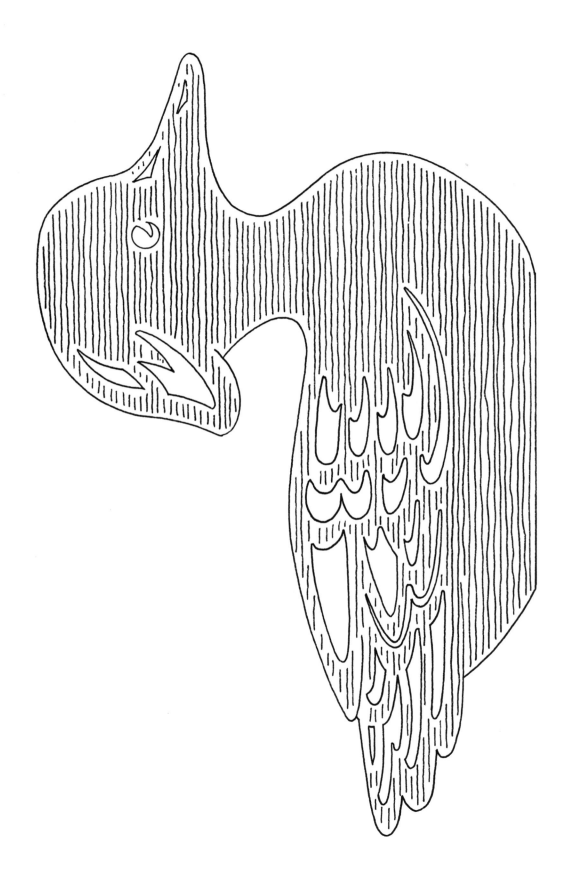

138

Fretted duck sawn from ½-inch thick Baltic-birch plywood.

Fretted loon made from ½-inch thick Baltic-birch plywood.

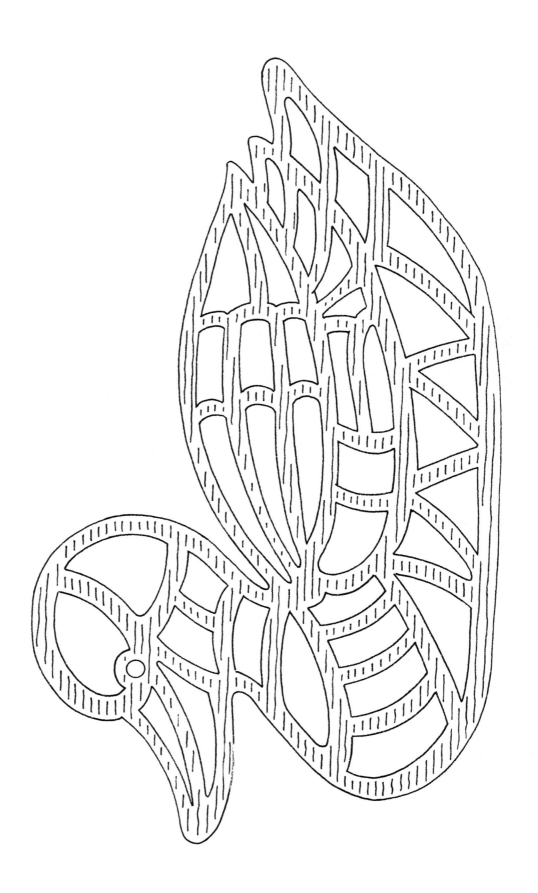

140

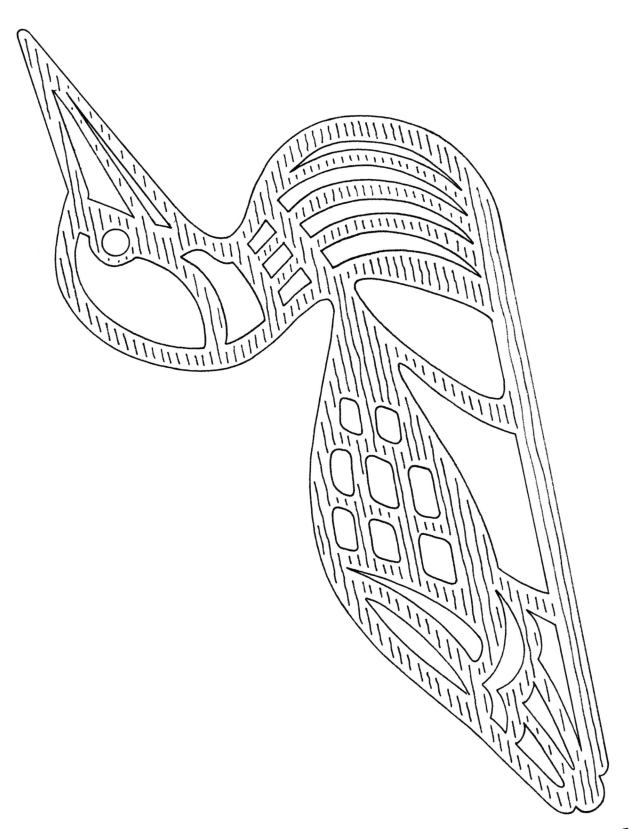

141

Mother loon sawn from ½-inch thick Baltic-birch plywood.

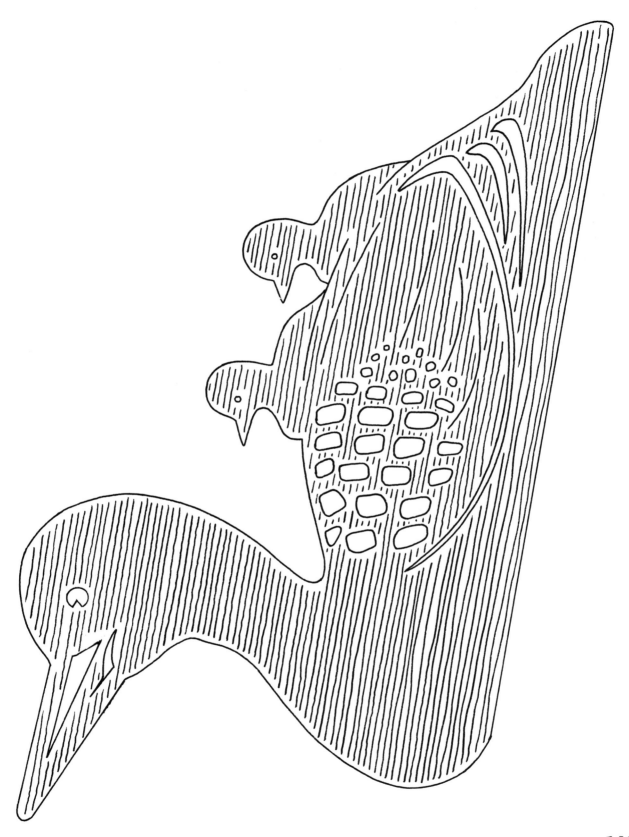

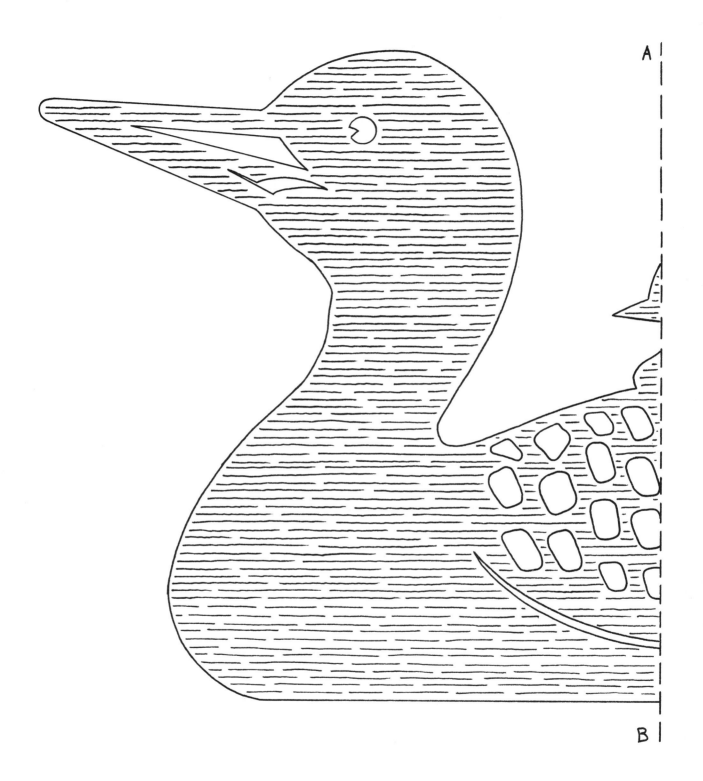

A

B

144

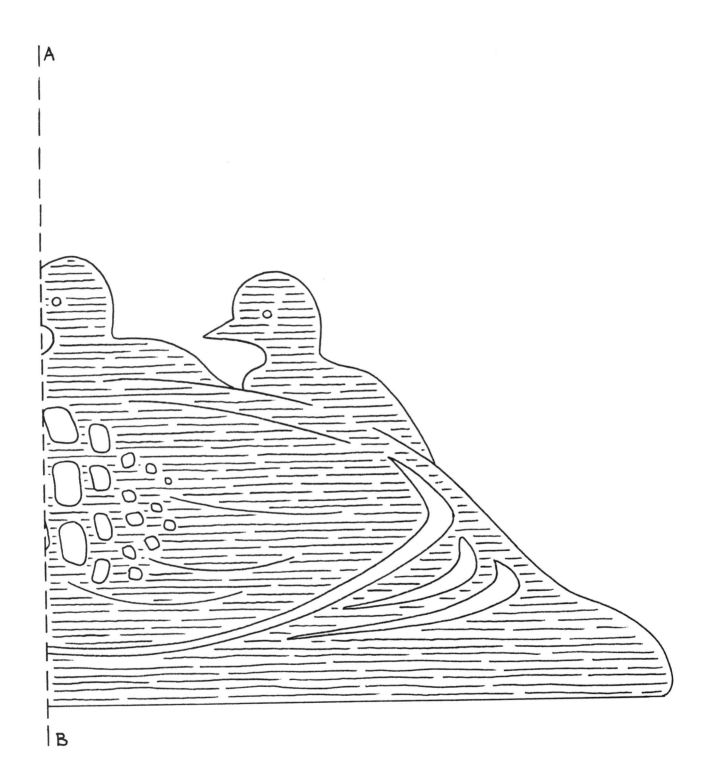

A

B

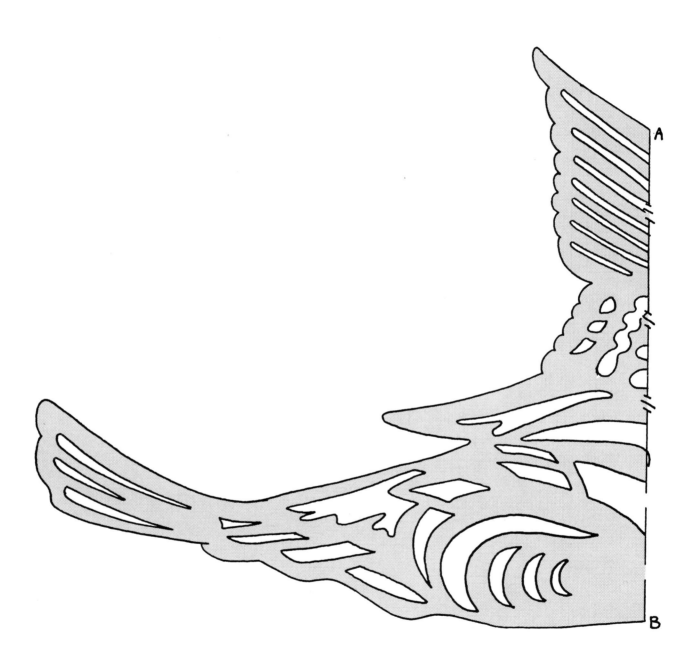

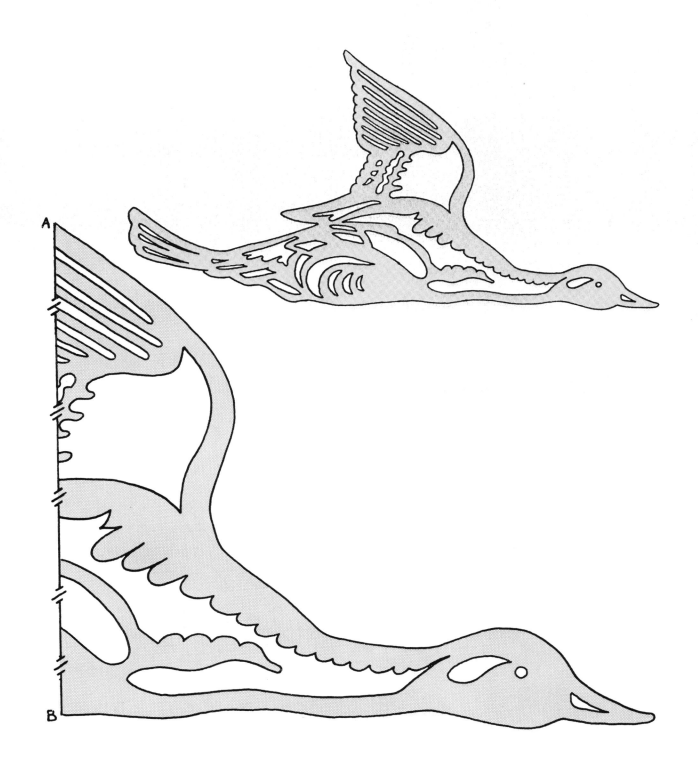

147

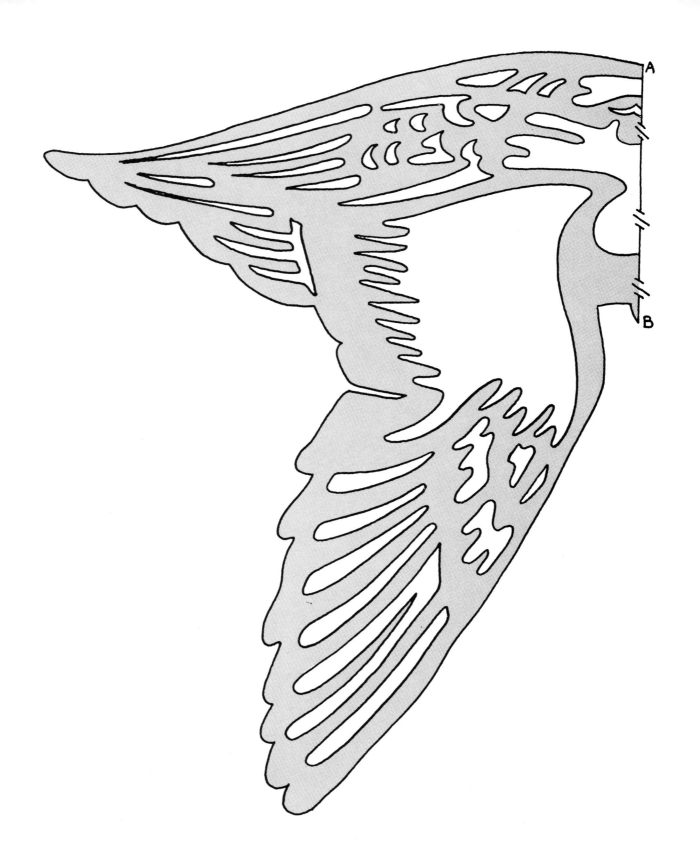

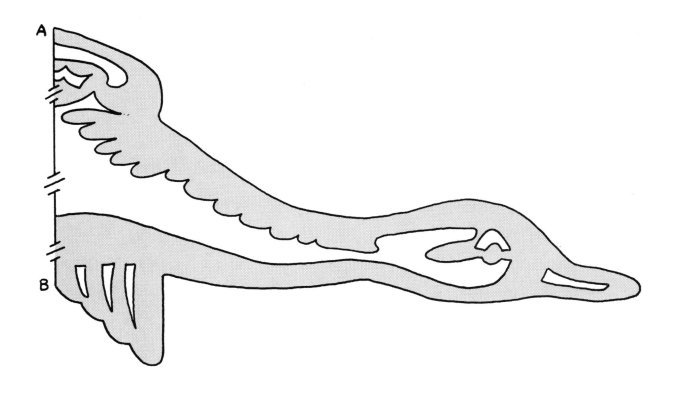

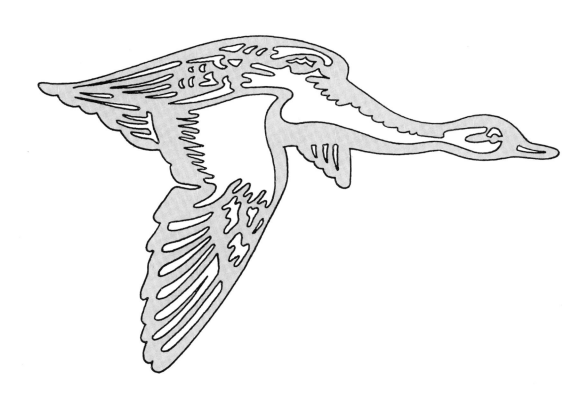

149

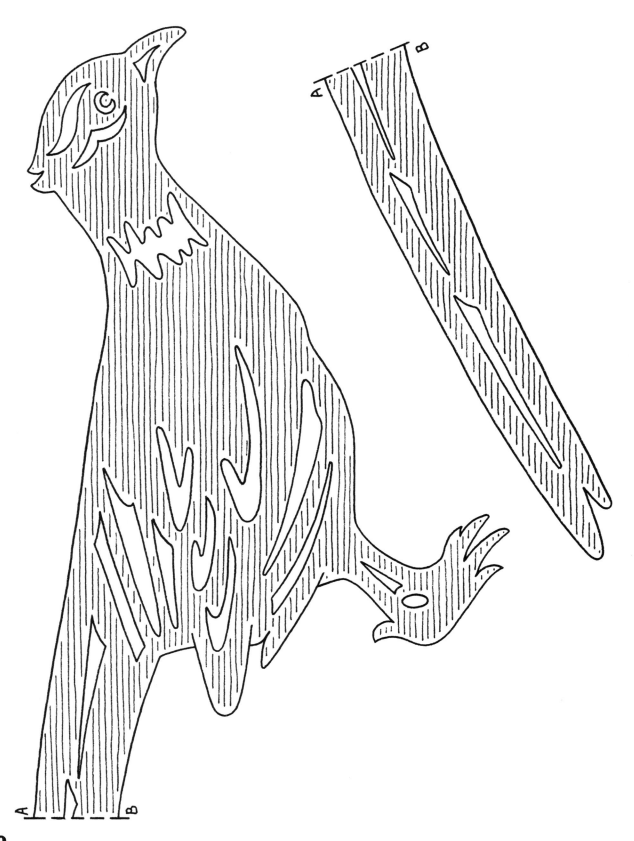

A

B

B

A

150

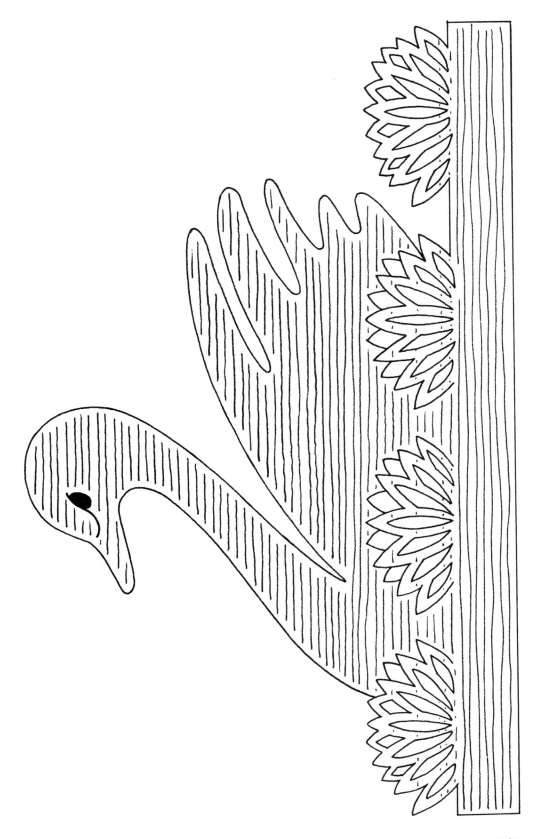

151

A

B

152

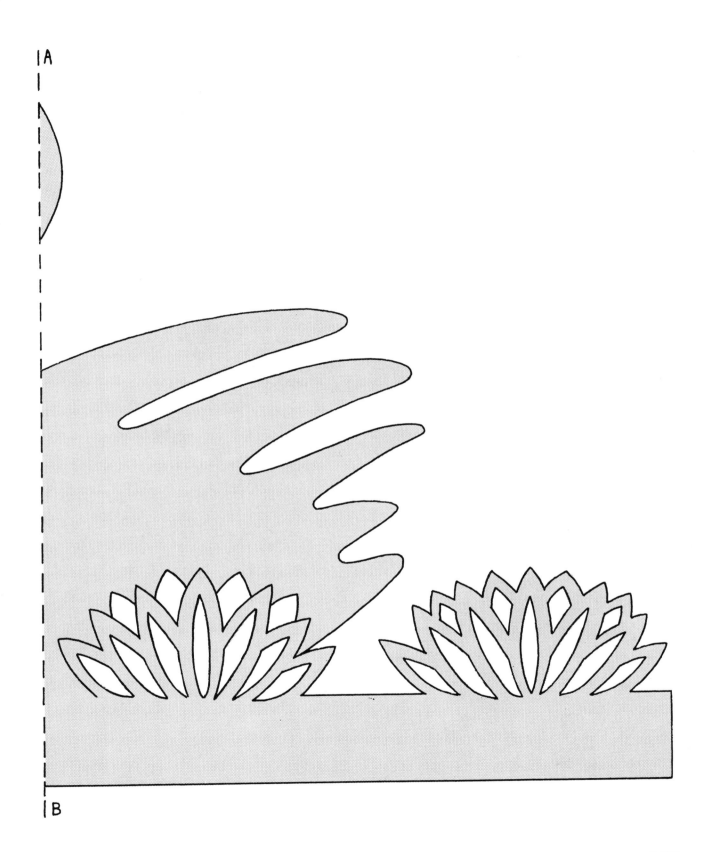

A

B

153

Fish and Sea Life

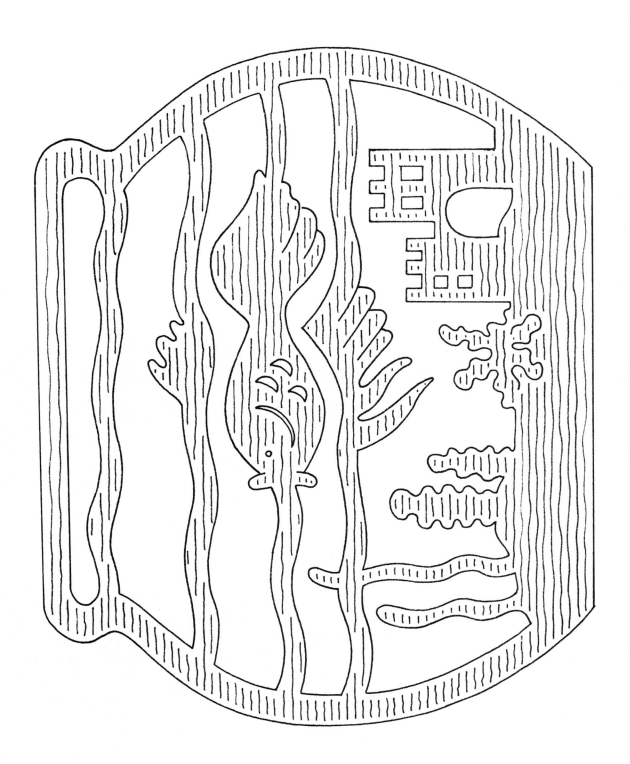

157

159

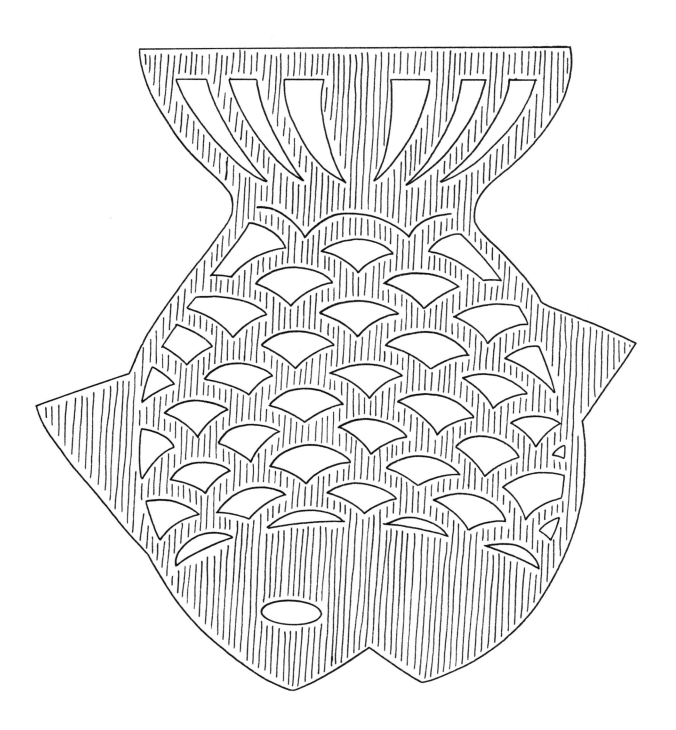

162

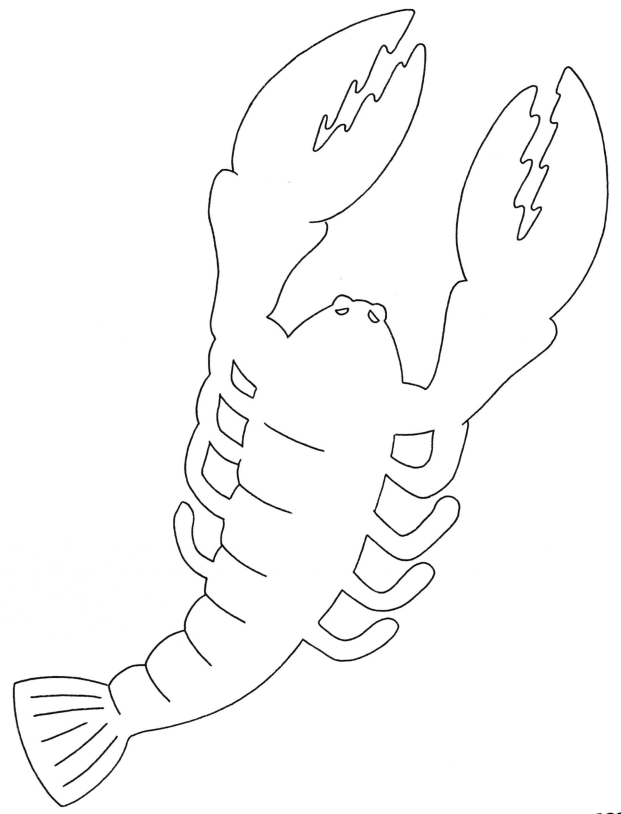

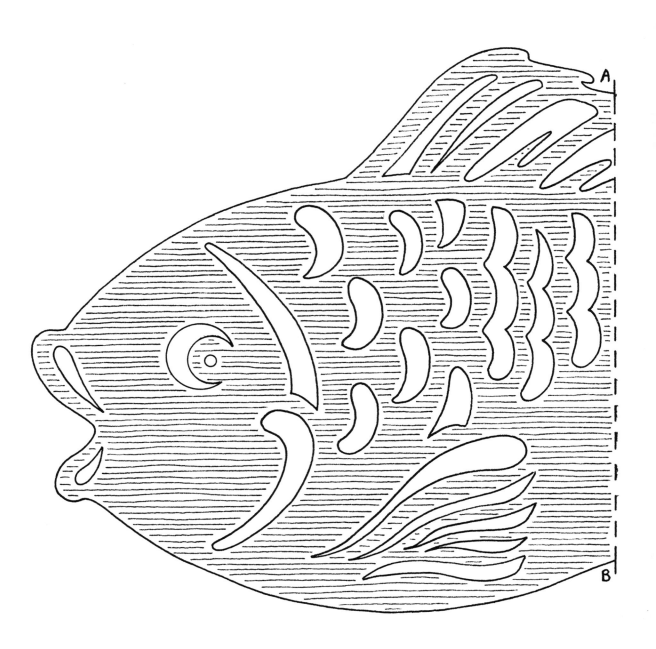

A

B

164

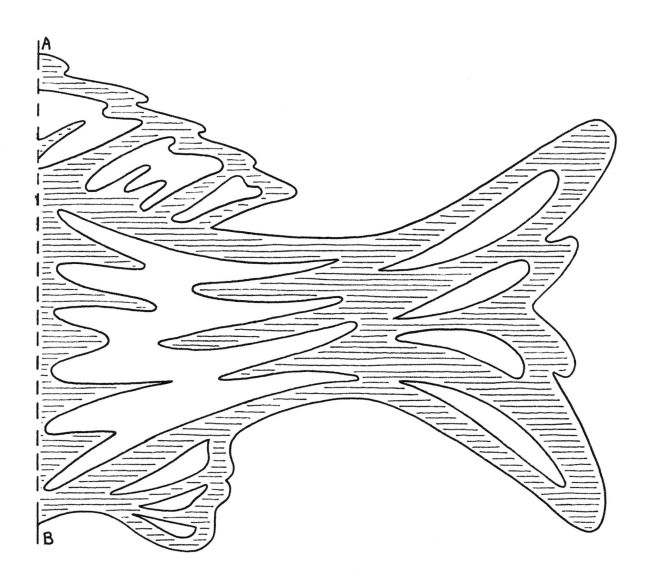

A

B

166

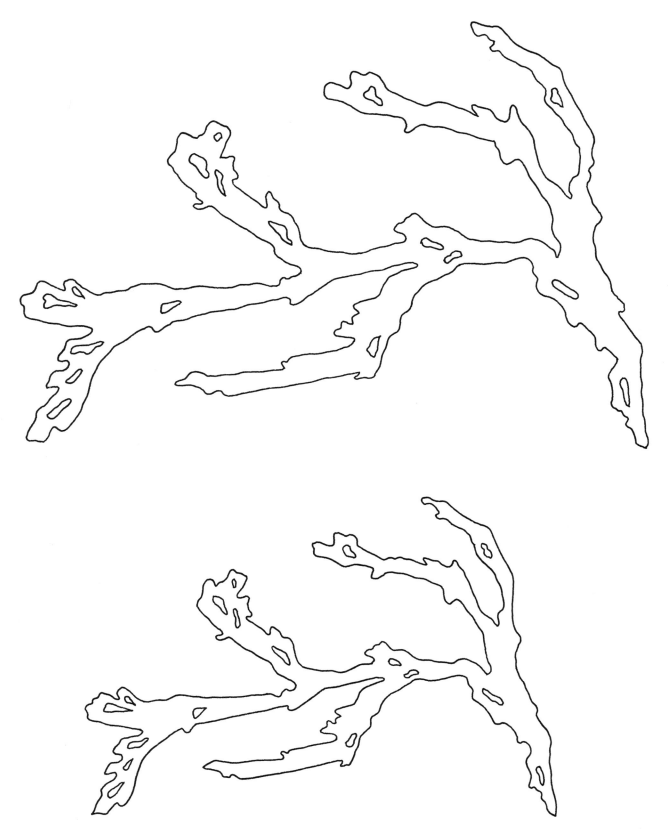

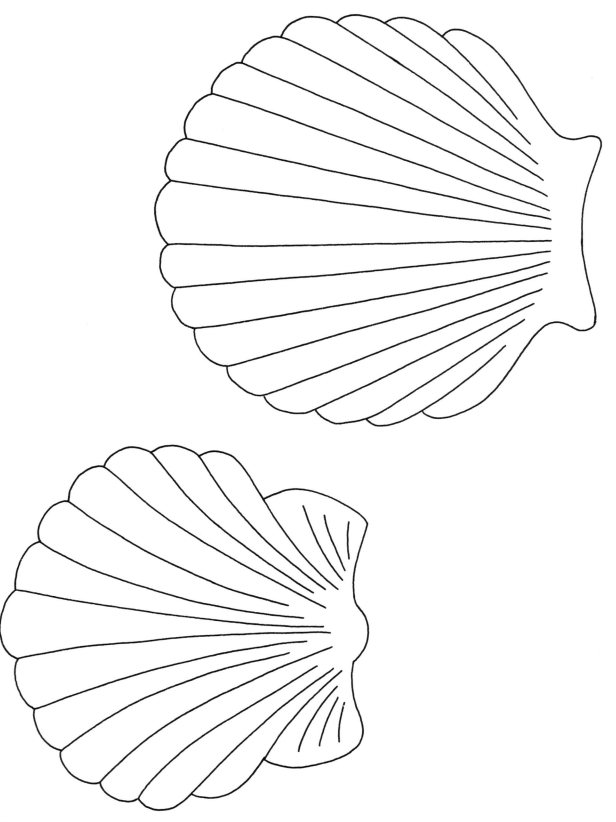

168

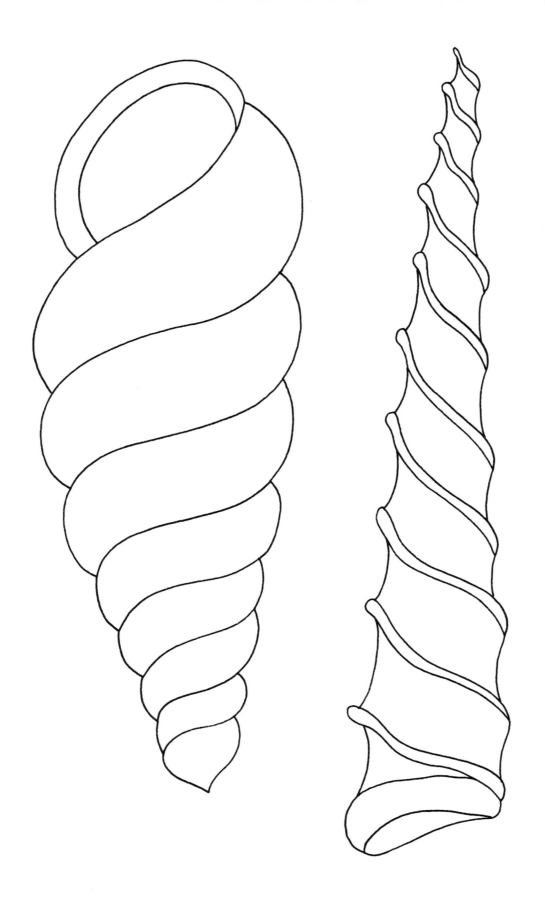

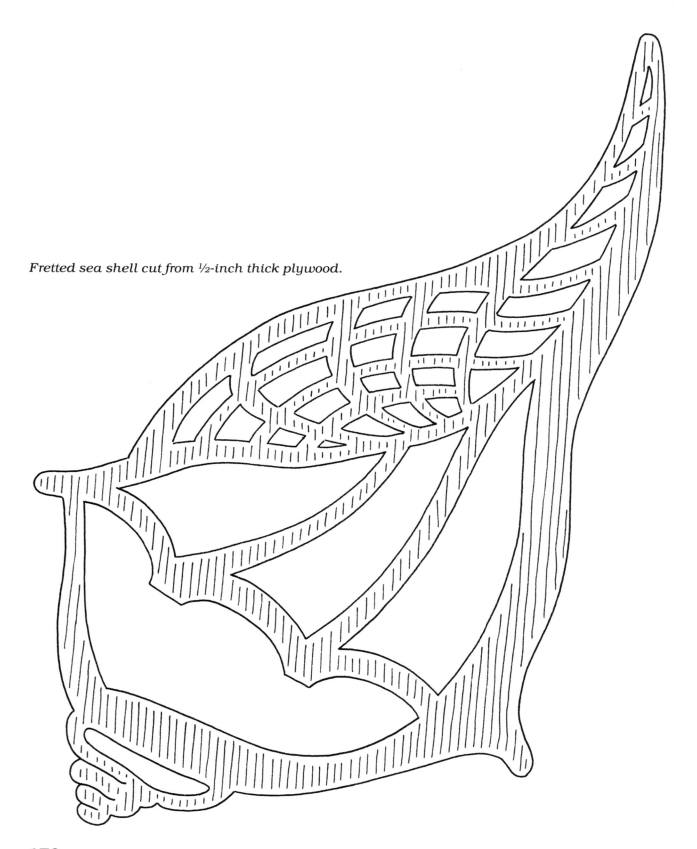

Fretted sea shell cut from ½-inch thick plywood.

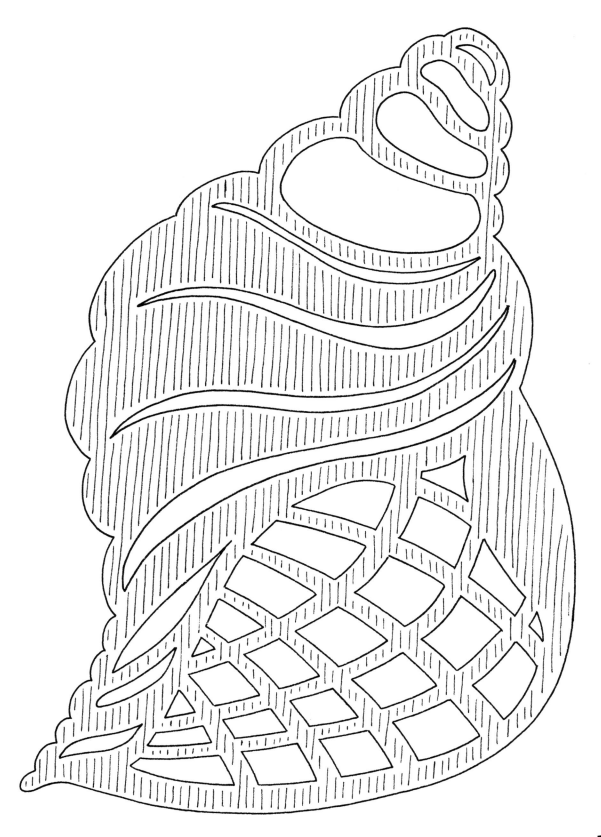

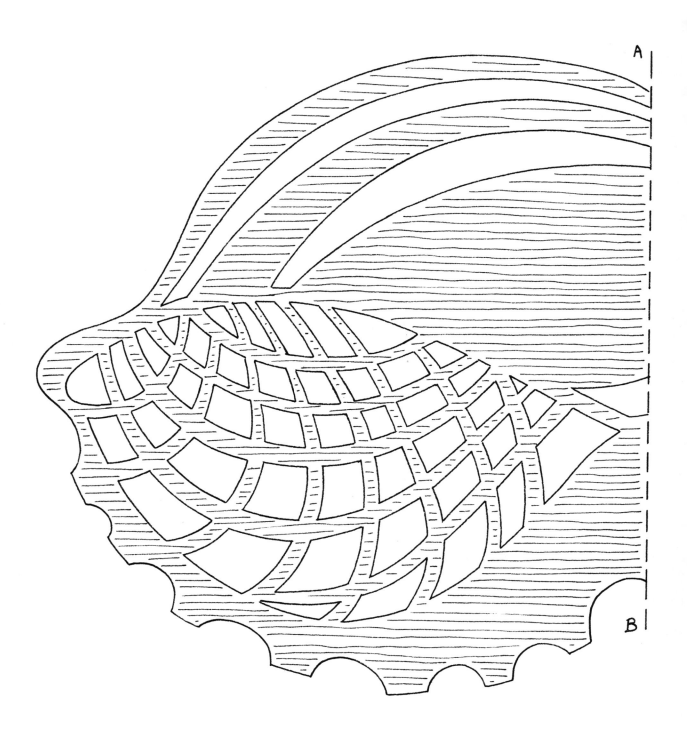

A

B

172

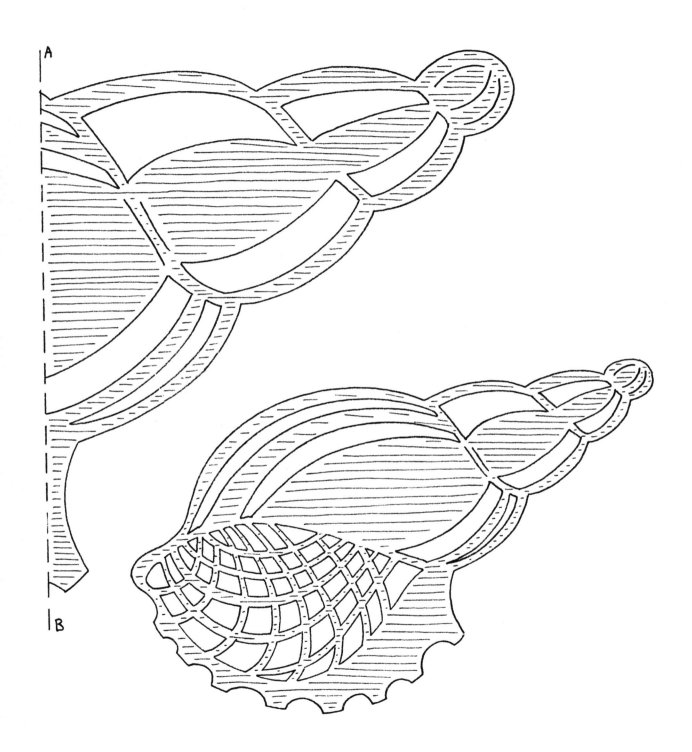

A

B

Flowers and Leaves

175

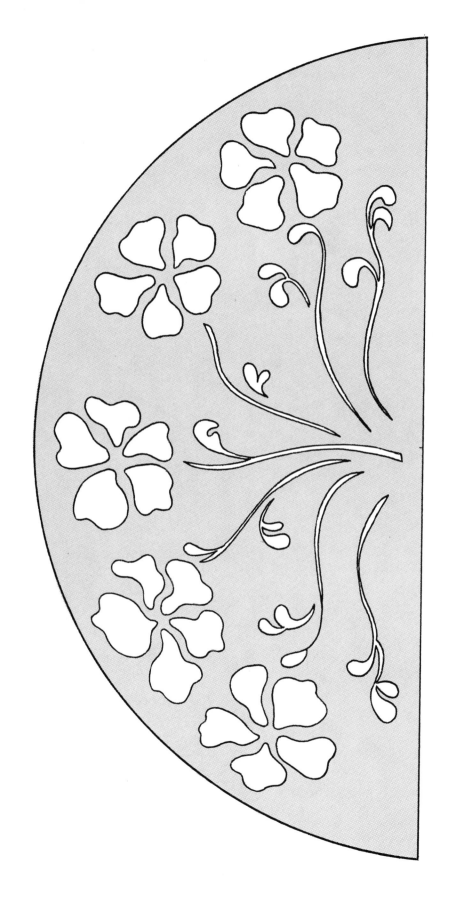

176

A

B

A

B

179

180

A

B

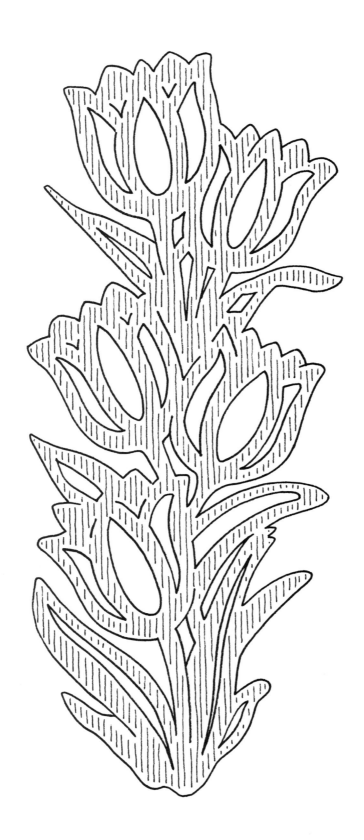

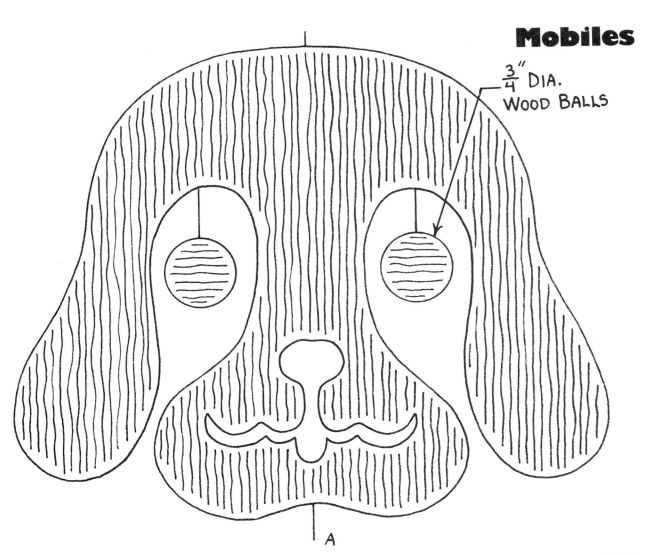

3/4" DIA. WOOD BALLS

A

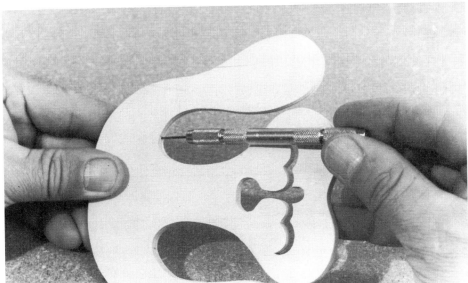

Puppy mobile sawn from thin (¼ inch) plywood.

Using a pin vise to drill a small hole in a hard-to-reach location. To hang ball eyes, insert fish line and glue it into the holes with a small wooden wedge such as the end of a toothpick.

184

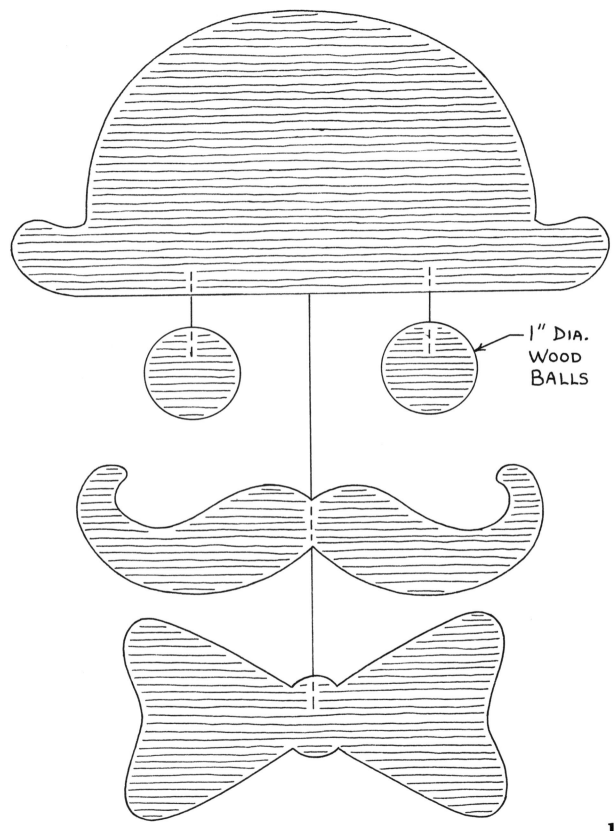

1" DIA.
WOOD
BALLS

185

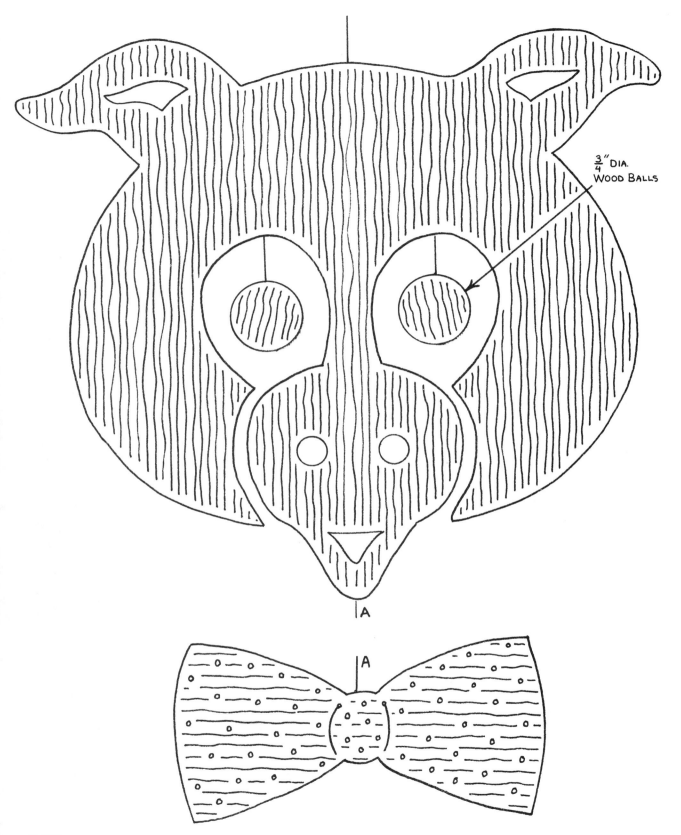

$\frac{3}{4}''$ DIA.
WOOD BALLS

A

A

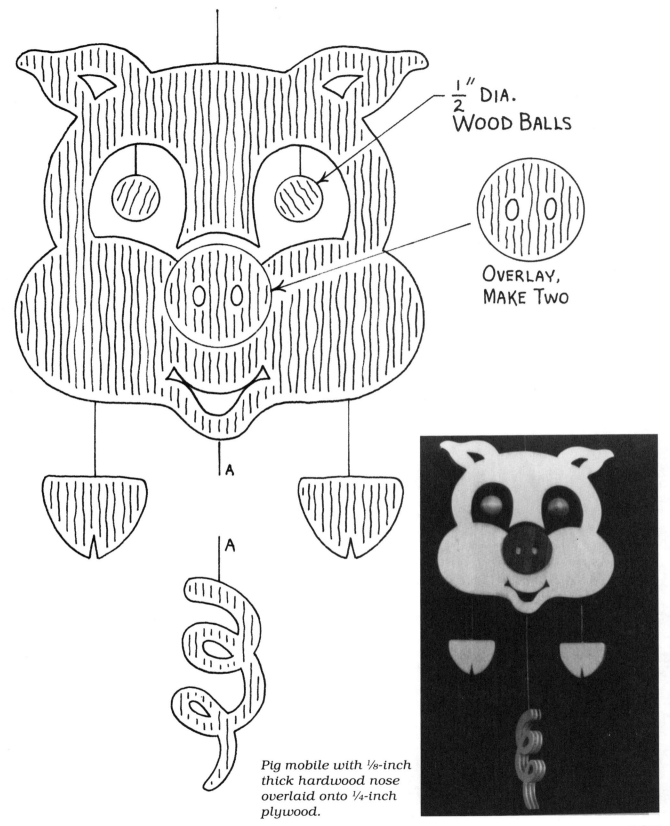

½" DIA.
WOOD BALLS

OVERLAY,
MAKE TWO

Pig mobile with ⅛-inch thick hardwood nose overlaid onto ¼-inch plywood.

187

½" DIA.
WOOD BALLS

A

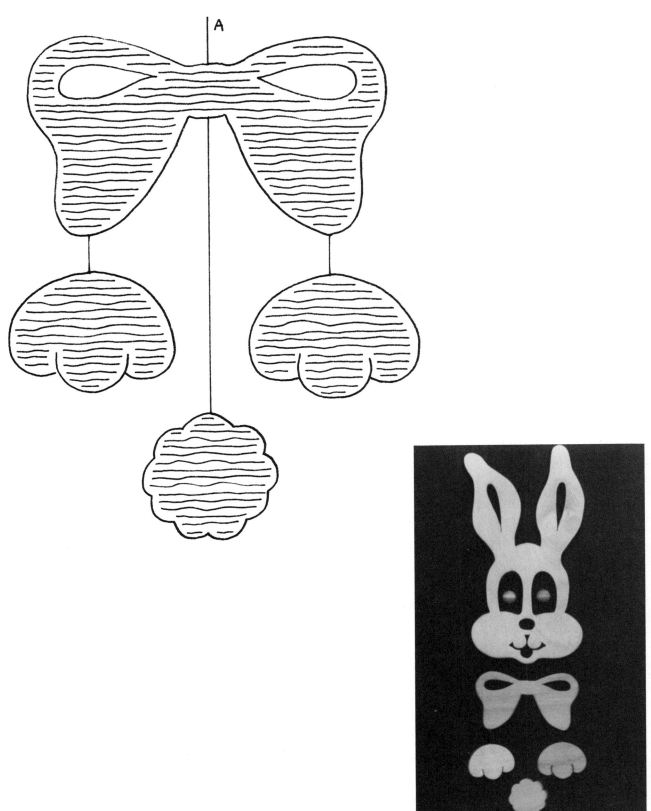

Rabbit mobile cut from ¼-inch plywood.

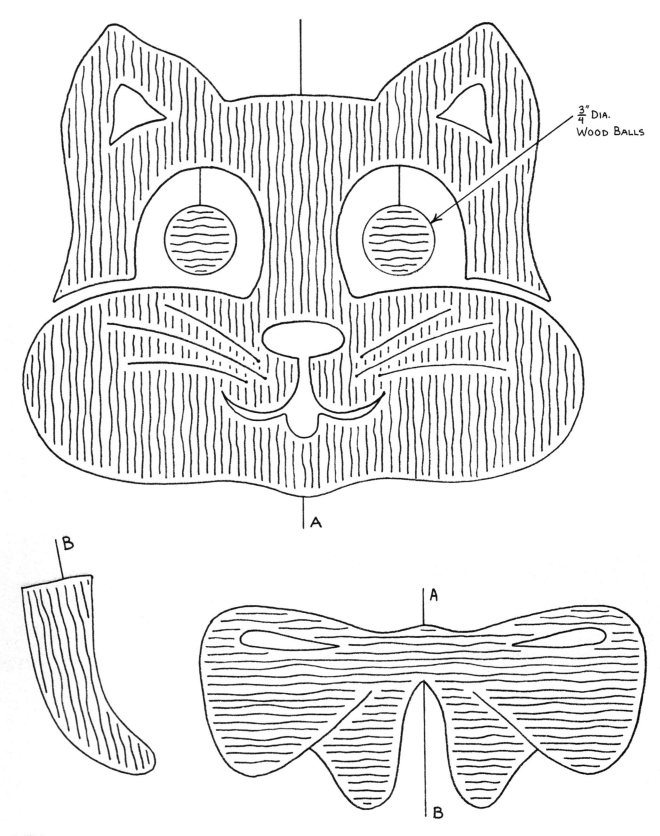

$\frac{3}{4}''$ DIA.
WOOD BALLS

A

B

A

B

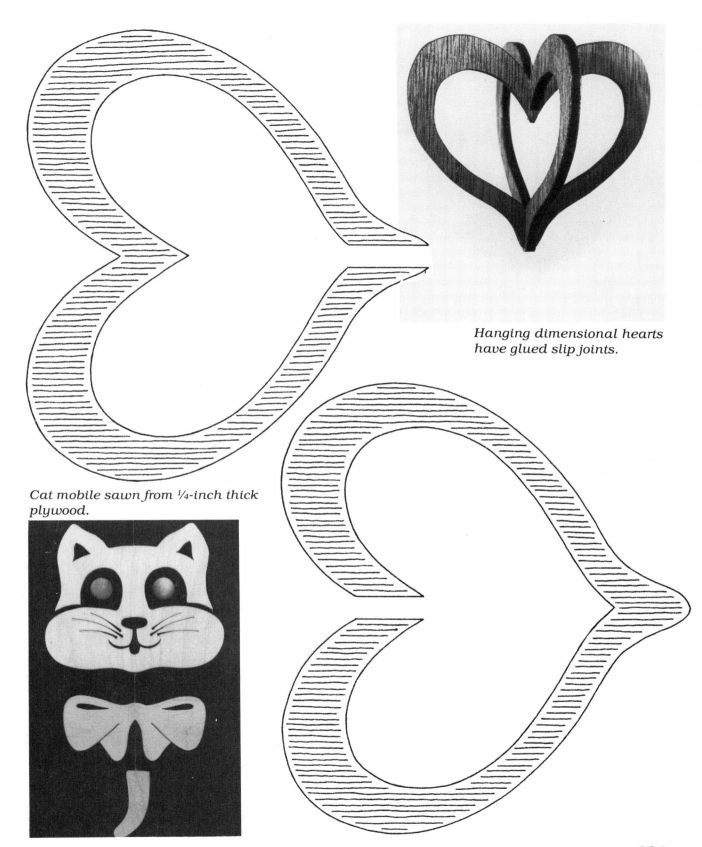

Hanging dimensional hearts
have glued slip joints.

Cat mobile sawn from ¼-inch thick
plywood.

Hanging heart mobile. The ¼-inch thick plywood parts are strung together on fine fish line.

196

197

199

200

201

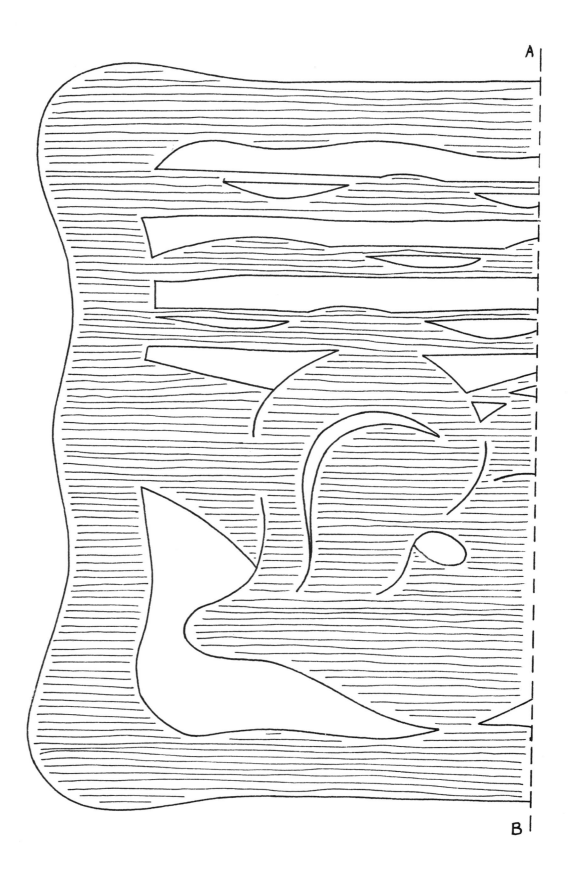

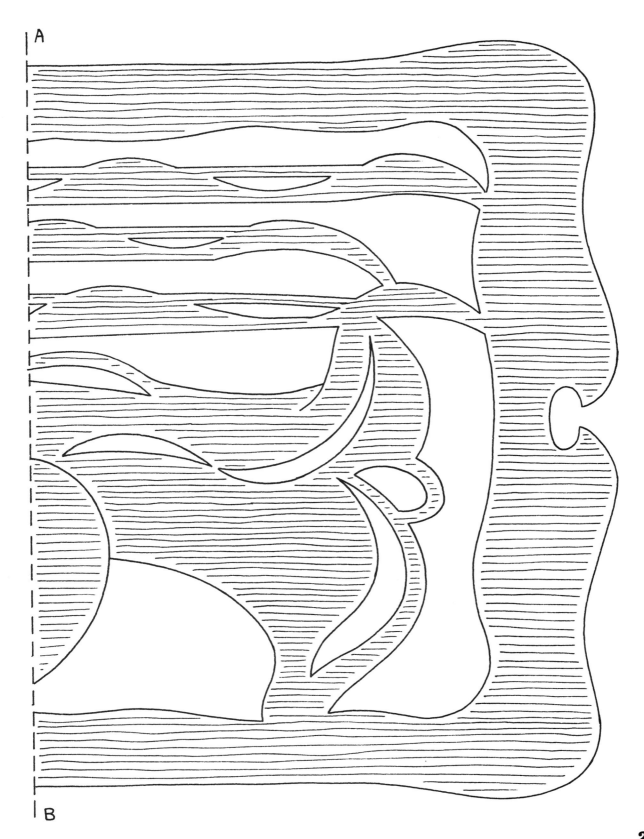

A

B

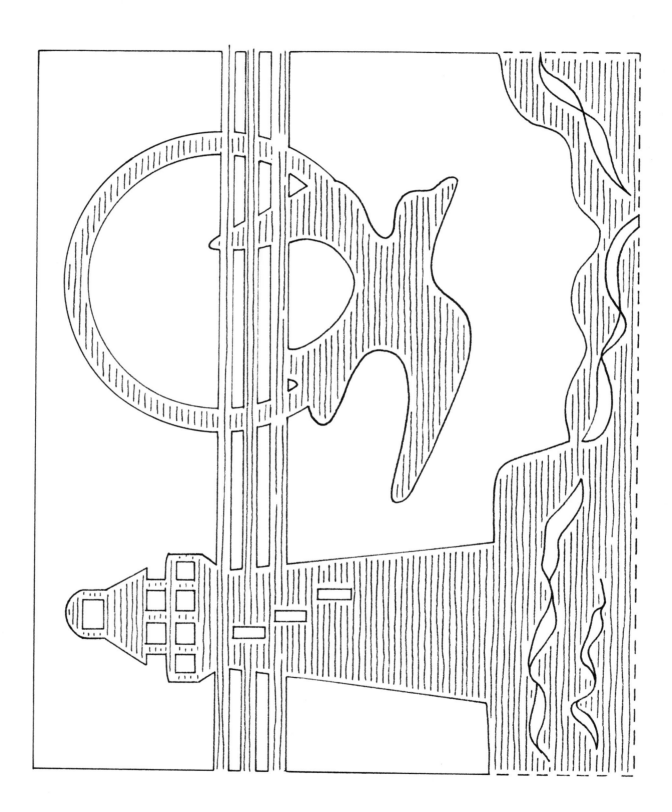

206

207

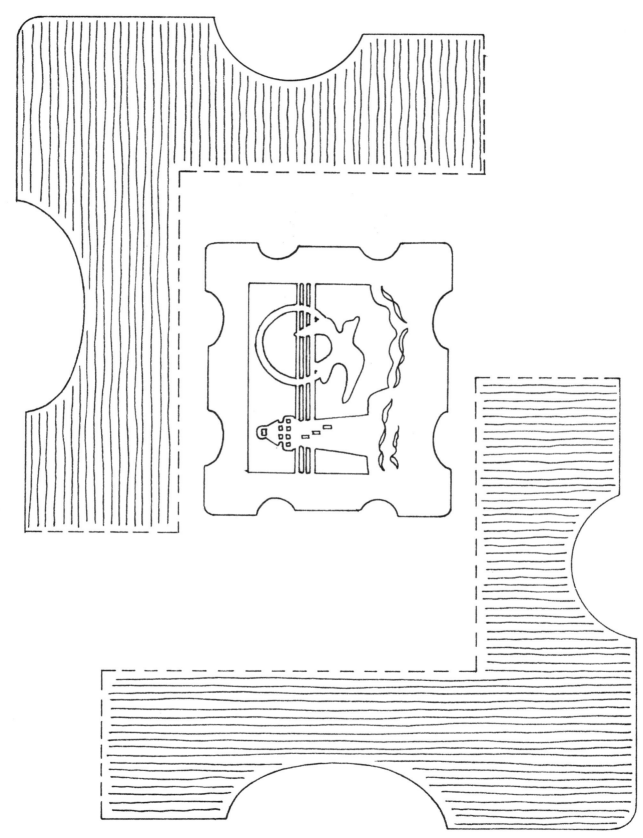

208

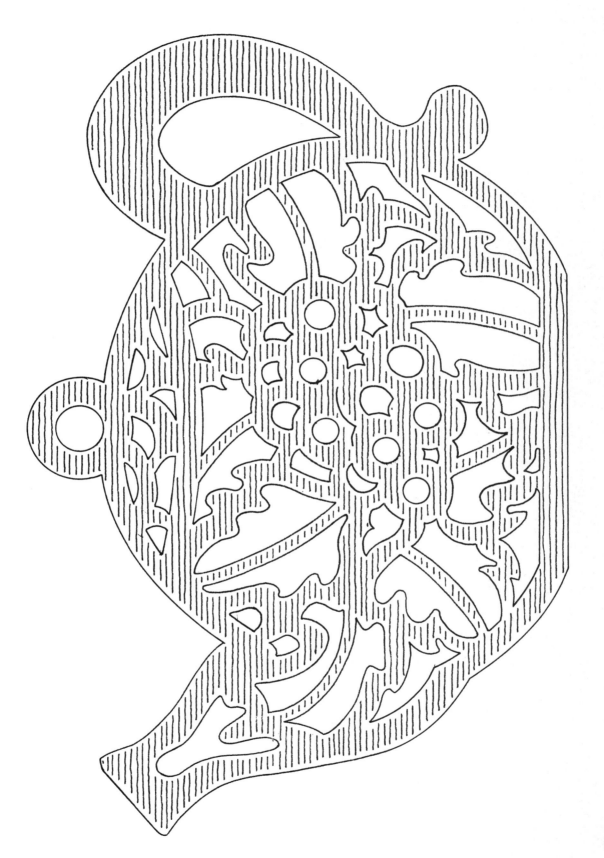

Wastebasket and Lamp

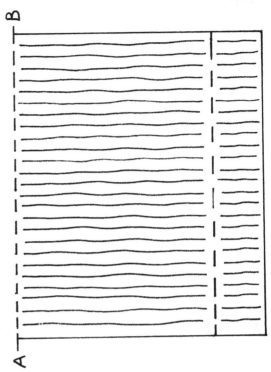

Octagon waste basket is made from ¼-inch thick butternut and features pierced panels, four of which are stack sawn.

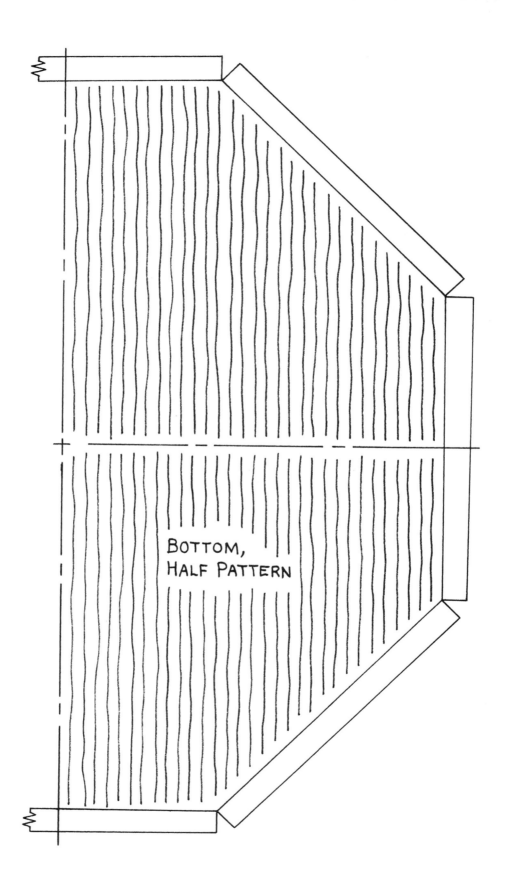

BOTTOM,
HALF PATTERN

This hanging lamp can be made with or without the roof-like top. As it is, it should only carry a very small bulb to keep heat at a minimum.

The hanging lamp without the top.

All six sides have been stacked and sawn at one time from stock previously ripped with 60°-beveled edges. Rubber bands are used to make a trial assembly and to provide the clamping pressure at glue-up.

The top slips onto the lamp cord and no other fastening is needed to hold it in place.

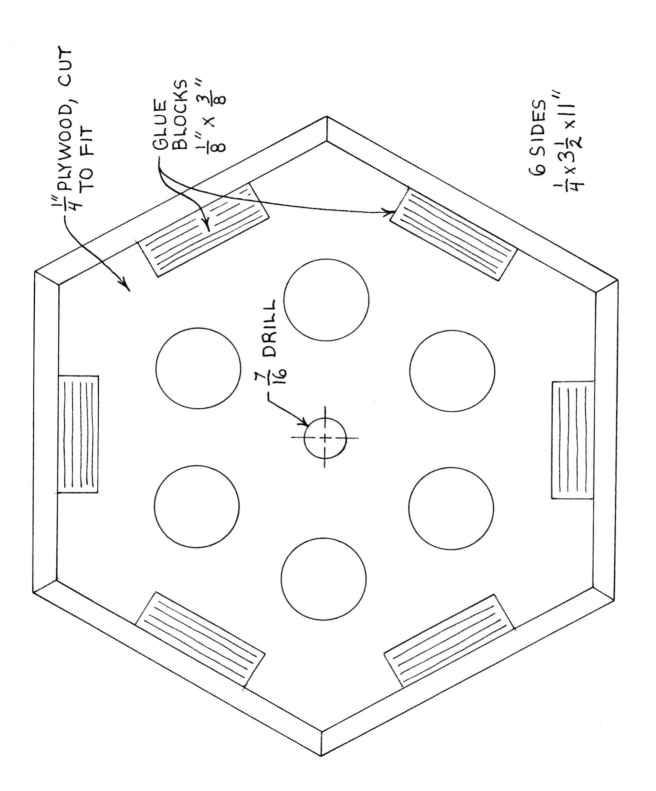

$\frac{1}{4}$" PLYWOOD, CUT TO FIT

GLUE BLOCKS $\frac{1}{8}$" × $\frac{3}{8}$"

6 SIDES $\frac{1}{4}$" × $3\frac{1}{2}$" × 11"

$\frac{7}{16}$ DRILL

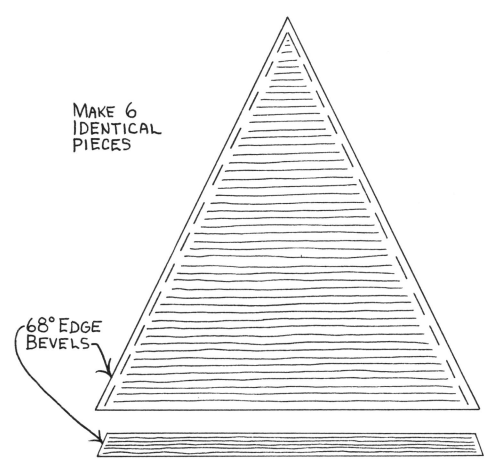

MAKE 6
IDENTICAL
PIECES

68° EDGE
BEVELS

This easy-to-make shooting board simplifies beveling the triangular top pieces. See the book, Scroll Saw Fretwork Techniques (Sterling Publishing), for details of how to make this shooting board.

The shooting board supports the work at the correct angle as it is cut with a sharp hand plane.

Six triangular parts for the top are taped together on the upper surfaces as shown.

Flip the taped top assembly cover and glue coat the edges that form the v-openings.

Tape holds the assembly together as the glue sets.

221

ABOUT THE AUTHORS

Patrick Spielman's love of wood began when, as a child, he transformed fruit crates into toys. Now this prolific and innovative woodworker is respected worldwide as a teacher and author.

His most famous contribution to the woodworking field has been his perfection of a method to season green wood with polyethylene glycol 1000 (PEG). He went on to invent, manufacture, and distribute the PEG-Thermovat chemical seasoning system.

During his many years as shop instructor in Wisconsin, Spielman published manuals, teaching guides, and more than 14 popular books, including *Modern Wood Technology*, a college text. He also wrote six educational series on wood technology, tool use, processing techniques, design, and wood-product planning.

Author of the best-selling *Router Handbook* (over 700,000 copies sold) and *Scroll Saw Pattern Book* (over 200,000 copies sold), Spielman has served as editorial consultant to a professional magazine, and his products, techniques, and many books have been featured in numerous periodicals. His works have also been translated into many foreign languages.

This pioneer of new ideas and inventor of countless jigs, fixtures, and designs used throughout the world is a unique combination of expert woodworker and brilliant teacher—all of which endear him to his many readers and to his publisher.

At Spielmans Wood Works in the woods of northern Door County, Wisconsin, he and his family create and sell some of the most durable and popular furniture products and designs available.

As both a buyer of wood products and the creator of Spielmans Wood Works Gift Shop and Gallery, Patricia Spielman ("Mrs. Pat") plays an invaluable part in the success of Spielmans Wood Works—and is well respected for his discerning eye for design and natural artistic ability.

Should you wish to write Pat or Patricia, please forward your letters to Sterling Publishing Company.

CHARLES NURNBERG
STERLING PUBLISHING COMPANY

CURRENT BOOKS BY PATRICK SPIELMAN

Alphabets and Designs for Wood Signs. 50 alphabet patterns, plans for many decorative designs, the latest on hand carving, routing, cutouts, and sandblasting. Pricing data. Photo gallery (4 pages in color) of wood signs by professionals from across the U.S. Over 200 illustrations. 128 pages.

Carving Large Birds. Spielman and renowned woodcarver Bill Dehos show how to carve a fascinating array of large birds. All of the tools and basic techniques that are used are discussed in depth, and hundreds of photos, illustrations, and patterns are provided for carving graceful swans, majestic eagles, comical-looking penguins, a variety of owls, and scores of other birds. Oversized. 16 pages in full color. 192 pages.

Carving Wild Animals: Life-Size Wood Figures. Spielman and renowned woodcarver Bill Dehos show how to carve more than 20 magnificent creatures of the North American wild. A cougar, black bear, prairie dog, squirrel, raccoon, and fox are some of the life-size animals included. Step-by-step, photo-filled instructions and multiple-view patterns, plus tips on the use of tools, wood selection, finishing, and polishing help you bring each animal to life. Oversized. Over 300 photos; 16 pages in full color. 240 pages.

Gluing & Clamping. A thorough, up-to-date examination of one of the most critical steps in woodworking. Spielman explores the features of every type of glue—from traditional animal-hide glues to the newest epoxies—the clamps and tools needed, the bonding properties of different wood species, safety tips, and all techniques from edge-to-edge and end-to-end gluing to applying plastic laminates. Also included is a glossary of terms. Over 500 illustrations. 256 pages.

Making Country-Rustic Wood Projects. Hundreds of photos, patterns, and detailed scaled drawings reveal construction methods, woodworking techniques, and Spielman's professional secrets for making indoor and outdoor furniture in the distinctly attractive Country-Rustic style. Covered are all aspects of furniture making from choosing the best wood for the job to texturing smooth boards. Among the dozens of projects are mailboxes, cabinets, shelves, coffee tables, weather vanes, doors, panelling, plant stands and many other durable and economical pieces. 400 illustrations. 4 pages in full color. 164 pages.

Making Wood Decoys. A clear step-by-step approach to the basics of decoy carving. This book is abundantly illustrated with closeup photos for designing, selecting, and obtaining woods; tools; feather detailing; painting; and finishing of decorative and working decoys. Six different professional decoy artists are featured. Photo gallery (4 pages in full color) along with numerous detailed plans for various popular decoys. 160 pages.

Making Wood Signs. Designing, selecting woods and tools, and every process through finishing are clearly covered. Hand-carved, power-carved, routed, and sandblasted processes in small to huge signs are presented. Foolproof guides for professional letters and ornaments. Hundreds of photos (4 pages in full color). Lists sources for supplies and special tooling. 144 pages.

Realistic Decoys. Spielman and master carver Keith Bridenhagen reveal their successful techniques for carving, feather-texturing, painting, and finishing wood decoys. Details that you can't find elsewhere—anatomy, attitudes, markings, and the easy step-by-step approach to perfect delicate procedures—make this book invaluable. Includes listings for contests, shows, and sources of tools and supplies. 274 closeup photos. 28 in color. 224 pages.

Router Handbook. With nearly 600 illustrations of every conceivable bit, attachment, jig, and fixture, plus every possible operation, this definitive guide has revolutionized router applications. It begins with safety and maintenance tips, then forges ahead into all aspects of dovetailing, free-handing, advanced duplication, and more. Details for over 50 projects are included. 224 pages.

Router Jigs & Techniques. A practical encyclopedia of information, covering the latest equipment to use with your router, it describes all the newest of commercial routing machines, along with jigs, bits, and other aids and devices. The book not only provides invaluable tips on how to determine the router and bits best suited to your needs, but tells you how to get the most out of your equipment once it is bought. Over 800 photos and illustrations. 384 pages.

Scroll Saw Fretwork Patterns. This companion book to *Scroll Saw Fretwork Techniques and Projects* features over 200 fabulous full-size fretwork patterns. These patterns include the most popular classic designs of the past, plus an array of imaginative contemporary ones. Choose from a variety of numbers, signs, brackets, animals, miniatures, and silhouettes, and many more. 256 pages.

Scroll Saw Fretwork Techniques and Projects. Spielman and master woodworker Reidle team up to make fretwork a quick and easy skill for anyone with access to a scroll saw, explaining every intricate detail in easy-to-follow instructions, photos, and drawings. Patterns for dozens of projects, make it easy for any scroll saw user to master these designs. 232 pages (8 in color).

Scroll Saw Handbook. This companion volume to *Scroll Saw Pattern Book* covers the essentials of this versatile tool, including the basics (how scroll saws work, blades to use, etc.) and the advantages and disadvantages of the general types and specific brand-name models available on the market. All cutting techniques are detailed, including compound and bevel sawing, making inlays, reliefs, and recesses, cutting metals and other non-woods, and marquetry. There's even a section on transferring patterns to wood! Over 500 illustrations. 256 pages.

Scroll Saw Pattern Book. This companion book to *Scroll Saw Handbook* contains over 450 workable patterns for making wall plaques, refrigerator magnets, candle holders, pegboards, jewelry, ornaments, shelves, brackets, picture frames, signboards, and many more projects. Beginners and experienced scroll saw users alike will find something to intrigue and challenge them. 256 pages.

Scroll Saw Puzzle Patterns. 80 full-size patterns for jigsaw puzzles, standup puzzles and inlay puzzles. With meticulous attention to detail, Patrick and Patricia Spielman provide instruction and step-by-step photos, along with tips on tools and wood selections, for making standup puzzles in the shape of dinosaurs, camels, hippopotamuses, alligators—even a family of elephants! Inlay puzzle patterns include basic shapes, numbers, an accurate piece-together map of the United States and a host of other colorful educational and enjoyable games for children. 8 pages of color. 256 pages.

Working Green Wood with PEG. Covers every process for making beautiful, inexpensive projects from green wood without cracking, splitting, or warping. Hundreds of clear photos and drawings show every step from obtaining the raw wood through shaping, treating, and finishing your PEG-treated projects. 175 unusual project ideas. Lists supply sources. 160 pages.

Index

Acorn, 115
airplane, 109
angel, Christmas, 105
antelope, 38
apple, 113, 114, 212

Ballerina, 72
bears, 45, 47
    small cutout, 21
    Teddy bears, 30–31
beaver, 37
bicycle rider, 69
birds, 117–126, 130–153
    framed cutout, 200–201, 209
    small cutouts, 20
boats
    framed cutout, 204–205
    Viking ship, 97
boxer, 70
buffalo, 39
bulldog, 87
bumble bee, 108
bunnies, 36, 88–90, 95–96,
        188–189
bus, 29
butterflies, 110–111

Cactus, 100–103
camel, 46
carolers, 34
cars, 27–29
cats, 80–83, 91–92
    framed cutout, 193
    mobile, 190
cherries, 115
cheetah, 50
chickens, 123
Christmas
    angel, 105
    carolers, 34
coffee pot cutout, 210
copying machines, 6–7
cows, 75
coyote, 104
crab, 166
crane cutout, 200
cutouts
    framed, 193–209
    fretted, 210–212

Dancers, 72–74
detailing line, 11–12
dinosaurs, 55–63
diver, 71
dogs, 80, 84–87, 93–94
    mobile, 183–184
dolphin, 154
double-faced tape, 14, 16

ducks, 117–118, 133–134,
        137–141, 143–145

Elephant, 40, 42, 44–46
    small cutout, 21

Face mobile, 185
fish, 154–162, 164–165
    framed cutout, 197
    small cutouts, 20
flamingo, 124–126
flowers and leaves, 174–182
    cutout, 199, 202–203
    framed cutout, 199
football player, 67
fox, 36
framed cutouts, 193–209
fretted cutouts, 210–212
frog, 116
fruit, 112–115

Geese, 120–121, 134–136,
        146–149
goldfish, 161–162
golfers, 64–66
grapes, 113
greyhound dog, 87

Hats, Vikings, 98
heart mobile, 191–192
heron, framed cutout, 200
hippopotamus, 40, 42, 48
horse and rider, framed cutout,
        194–195
horses, 76–79
hummingbird, 131

Indians, 24
inside cutting, 12

Jack in the box, 23

Kelp, 167

Lambs, 22
lamp, 215–221
leaves and flowers, 174–182
leopard, 51
lighthouse scene, framed cutout,
        206–208
lion, 41, 48, 49, 50–51, 53
lobster, 163
loon, 141, 143

Marlin, 155
mice, 25–26
mobiles, 183–192
monkey, small cutout, 21
mushrooms, 106–107
musical cutouts, 32–35

Nuts, 115

Outdoors scene, cutout, 196
owl, small cutout, 21

Palm tree, 127
patterns, see also specific
        patterns
    general overview of, 9–17
pear, 113
penguins, 18–19
pheasants, 150
piercing, 12, 17
pig
    mobile, 186–187
    small cutout, 21
plural sawing, 14–16
porpoise, 159

Rabbits, 36, 88–90, 95–96
    mobile, 188–189
racoon, 39
ram, 52
retriever, 87
rhinoceros, 41
roosters, 122, 128–129

Scene, framed cutout, 196
scottie dog, 80, 87
scroll sawing, popularity of, 6–8
sea life, 163–173
shark, 159
shells, 168–173
skier, 68, 198
skunk, 38
small cutouts, 20–21
Southwestern cutouts, 99–104
sports figures, 64–71
spray adhesive, 7–8
squirrel, 37
stack cutting, 14–17
starfish, 166
swans, 151–153
swordfish, 160

Tea pot cutout, 211
Teddy bears, 30–31
tiger, 48, 49
toy cutouts, 27–29
tractors, 28
trucks, 27–29
turkeys, 119

Viking ship, 97–98

Wastebasket, 213–214
wildcat, 50
wildlife, 36–54